GRANITE SKIES

Renee,
Thanks so much for supporting this project. Keep looking up!

Granite Skies: A Disconcerted Journey Through the Unknown © 2020 by Nomar Slevik. All rights reserved. No part of this book may be used or reproduced in any manner, including Internet usage, without written permission from Nomar Slevik, except in the case of brief quotations embodied in critical articles and reviews.

First Edition
Second Printing, 2020

Book Cover designed by Mark Randall
Edited by Valerie Lofaso
Book Layout by Nomar Slevik
Interior photos supplied by author & Mike Stevens

Library of Congress Cataloging-in-Publication Data (Pending)
ISBN: 979-8-6224-2190-7

Any Internet references contained in this work are current at publication time, but Nomar Slevik cannot guarantee that a specific location will continue to be maintained.

Printed in the United States of America

About the Author
Nomar Slevik is an independent creator, researcher and investigator in numerous aspects of the paranormal. He delights in sharing stories through different mediums such as books, documentaries and podcasts. He has shared his works with hundreds of thousands of enthusiasts and has maintained a steady output of material for over twenty years.

Slevik has been fascinated by all things paranormal since childhood, beginning with a UFO encounter at 4 years old. Now 42, his life's passion has been to research, investigate, write, and share UFO and extraterrestrial encounters from everyday people in a way that conveys the human element of profoundly strange encounters.

To Write the Author
If you wish to send correspondence or would like more information about this book, feel free to email the author directly.

Nomar Slevik
slevik@gmail.com

Granite Skies
A Disconcerted Journey Through the Unknown

Nomar Slevik

Foreword by Valerie Schultz

ACKNOWLEDGEMENTS

First, a big, loud thank you to Mike Stevens and his willingness to tell his story no matter what. His honesty is forever admired. - Valerie Lofaso, my editor, colleague and friend; endless thank yous for your hard work with this book. - Malik Abdul Fattah, love you like a son. You're in my heart forever, lil homie. - Kyle Sawyer, your friendship when I was at my lowest knew no bounds. I love you, buddy. - Shauna & Josh, yall saved my life without even trying. Thank you for showing me what love can be. - Mindy Bolduc, you were a friend when it felt like there were none. - April, what can I say? Always in my heart. - Katie, you made me believe in possibilities again. - Stephanie Kelley Romano, you're a warrior and a beacon of positivity. Thank you for being you. - Susan Ahlin, you taught me so much and showed me a type of kindness that I forgot existed. - Bill Brock, collaborating with you helped me to trust collaborators again. - Andrea, the confidence you have in my work holds me over when I have none of my own. - Erik Cooley, your support of me has never wavered, thank you. - Scott & Kim, you're my brother and sister. I'm so happy that we reconnected. - Valerie Schultz, thank you for always believing in me. - And to my family, you believe in not only the work I do, but in me as a person. You are loved.

DEDICATION

Dedicated to all the survivors. You are seen and you are heard. This is also for the ones who did not make it. We remember you.

CONTENTS

Foreword   11

Introduction   15

As Above, So Blue Infant (1979)   22

Strange Invaders (1983)   32

Betty and Barney and Beyond   49

Intruders (1987-1990)   70

Dreamcatcher (1991-1992)   81

Picture Section   90

The Chronicles of Nonsense (1994-1998)   103

Silver Linings (2000-2006)   112

Stranger Things (2010-2015)   139

How It All Ends (2016-Present)   160

Epilogue   182

Bibliography   186

Foreword

As a MUFON Field Investigator and State Director for New Hampshire and Maine, I have investigated and researched several hundred UFO cases since 2012. As a result, it seems obvious to me that there is so much we really don't know about UFOs and the paranormal.

MUFON's mission statement is "the scientific study of UFOs for the benefit of humanity." MUFON Investigators are all volunteers doing their part to help discover the truth about UFOs. MUFON is the oldest UFO organization in the world, having begun in 1969 and we just celebrated our 50th Anniversary in 2019. We have an online database of over 100,000 cases that have been submitted to us worldwide. As researchers and investigators, we look for commonalities in our submitted reports, local hotspots and sighting trends.

Many people are surprised to hear that I've never seen a UFO. In spite of that, my curiosity has sparked many questions about our surroundings, our limited scientific knowledge and our universe. That curiosity and pursuit of information eventually brought me to MUFON.

All my life I've looked at the stars and wondered how many planets out there could be teeming with life. I pondered the thought of how many different varieties of life existed in other galaxies. The universe is so vast, how could we possibly be alone? The thought that the Earth is the only place with intelligent life always seemed arrogant to me so I began reading books by John Keel, Frank Edwards, Timothy Beckley and more. They helped me to open my mind and made me question everything.

When I started following Stanton Friedman's works, I realized that if a real scientist, a nuclear physicist and MUFON member, was researching UFO sightings and believed that some sightings were from off planet, then I could follow that path too. Stanton Friedman was best known for his work with the Betty and Barney Hill case and the Roswell Incident. He was known as "The Father of Modern-Day Ufology." I spoke to Stanton Friedman several times and he was always so kind and approachable. When he passed in 2019, the world lost an awesome advocate for the truth about UFOs and I lost a hero of mine.

New Hampshire MUFON

Researching and investigating so many cases

submitted to New Hampshire MUFON, I've discovered some commonalities, trends, and hotspots. For the time period 2012 – 2019, New Hampshire MUFON received 349 cases. Here is the breakdown of reports submitted by county for that time period: Belknap 76, Rockingham 69, Hillsborough 52, Merrimack 36, Strafford, Grafton and Coos 25 each, Carroll 20, Cheshire 16, and Sullivan 5. Although Belknap, Rockingham and Hillsborough Counties have the most reported sightings, the most interesting, unusual and compelling cases have arrived from Coos and Grafton Counties.

New Hampshire MUFON has received sightings of silent and slow-moving football field and aircraft carrier sized triangular crafts and various sized disc-shaped crafts. Most sightings are silent but we've had several reports of electric-type hums. Craft have been described as gliding or levitating and some craft have affected car engines and radios. We recently received a fascinating report of a massive, metallic, disc-shaped craft that hovered in the vicinity of Canobie Lake Park in 1964. Sphere, circle, and triangular shaped craft have been reported the most over the last 8 years. Of those 349 cases submitted to New Hampshire MUFON since 2012, 129 were closed as "unknown".

Granite Skies

With this book, "Granite Skies: A Disconcerted Journey Through the Unknown," Nomar Slevik will discuss some famous New Hampshire UFO encounters such as the Betty and Barney Hill incident and the Exeter encounter. However, the main focus of this book will lead you through the life and unusual encounters of a New Hampshire man named Mike Stevens, someone well known to New Hampshire UFO experiencers. I salute Mr. Stevens for his strength in sharing his story and for his perseverance in creating the petition that led to the historical marker on Route 3 in Lincoln, New Hampshire that commemorates the location of the Betty and Barney Hill abduction. Well done and thank you Mike Stevens!

Nomar Slevik's first two books: "UFOs Over Maine: Close Encounters from the Pine Tree State" and "Otherworldly Encounters: Evidence of UFO Sightings and Abductions", were very informative, enlightening, and a pleasure to read. I know you will be captivated by the compelling and insightful information in this book.

Valerie Schultz
MUFON State Director
for New Hampshire and Maine
January 31, 2020

Introduction

It was August 31, 2018 when I began this writing. It also happened to be just one day before the 9th annual Exeter UFO Festival was to commence. It was a late afternoon and I was seated at a desk in the hotel room of a Hampton Inn located in Exeter, New Hampshire. I wanted to write down my thoughts before giving a presentation that evening at the KRI Center for Consciousness Studies located just up the road in Stratham. The next day would bring me back to Maine to begin shooting a documentary about a couple who had been experiencing ongoing, seemingly extraterrestrial encounters. Because of that shoot, I would miss Exeter's two-day otherworldly party.

The festival first launched in 2010 and has attracted prominent lecturers in ufology such as Peter

Robbins, Kathleen Marden, Richard Dolan, Stanton Friedman, and more. The event is a fundraising benefit for local children's charities and, after almost a decade, draws thousands of visitors from across the country and has become the Exeter Area Kiwanis Club's major fundraising event of the year. So, why does such a thing happen in Exeter, New Hampshire? According to the *Exeter UFO Festival* website "The festival is held in Exeter in part because of a famous 1965 incident where a UFO was seen flying around." The incident being referred to is that of an encounter experienced by one man and two police officers.

In the early morning hours of September 3, 1965, a young man named Norman Muscarello walked along Highway 150 toward his parent's home (technically in the town of Kensington, which is just a hair over the border from Exeter), hoping to catch a ride. As Norman walked, he observed a handful of flashing red lights in the woods. He stared at them in frightened fascination and, in his opinion, the lights seemed to notice him and moved toward his direction.

He jumped into a nearby ditch to hide, but the lights found no interest in Norman and hovered over a nearby farmhouse for a moment before they retreated into the woods. As soon as the lights were gone, Norman ran to the farmhouse for help, but his knocking went unanswered. Scared, he headed back to the road in the hopes that a car would soon come by. Headlights approached and Norman stood in the middle of the road to get the driver's attention. The car slowed, the young man was frantic and asked to be taken to the police station. The occupants, an older couple, saw how frightened he was and agreed to drive him.

Norman appeared genuinely frightened as he told his story to the officer behind the counter. The officer did not fully understand it all but believed something happened to Norman and radioed a colleague that was on patrol. Officer Bertrand arrived at the station minutes later to hear the story for himself. It was then decided that the two, Bertrand and Norman, would go back to the farmhouse area to investigate. Once on site, the men noticed animals on the farm acting in an agitated state. Moments later, the pair observed a large object with red flashing lights ascend out of the woods and head toward them. The men dropped to the ground in an attempt to hide from the lights; Bertrand then drew his gun and aimed it at the object. From the nose of the weapon, he stared at the oddity in awe. He holstered the gun as he knew it would be useless against the aerial phenomenon. Both men retreated to the police car and Bertrand radioed another officer on patrol that evening. Officer Hunt arrived quickly and gawked at the object with the other two men. After a moment, the object took off over the woods and out of sight. Seconds later, all three men observed a B-47 bomber roar past them toward the direction the object went. The shaken men drove back to the Exeter police station in silence, most likely trying to process what they had witnessed. All three men filed reports on what they saw and their story went national.

The Air Force showed interest in the case and sent two of their officers to interview the witnesses. Major David Griffin and Lieutenant Alan Brandt spoke with the three men and described them in their report as "stable and reliable" and "found nothing in the area that could be probable cause." The Air Force, under pressure from increasing media inquiries, reported to the press that the event was simply misidentification of "stars and planets twinkling" and "temperature inversion". Despite the Air Force press release, Project Blue Book (studies and investigations of UFOs conducted by the Air Force) reported that what the men had witnessed was a training mission by NORAD called Operation Big Blast.

After hearing Project Blue Book's explanation, the three witnesses vehemently disagreed with the findings, and the officers wrote letters to Project Blue Book in protest. Getting no response, the men then worked with journalist John G. Fuller and Raymond Fowler (who was a member of NICAP, the National Investigations Committee on Aerial Phenomena). Between the five of them, they were able to publish their own findings which was in stark contrast to the Air Force's report. Finally, in January of 1966, some four months after the encounter, a Lieutenant Colonel from "the Office of the Secretary of the Air Force" replied to the men's letters written to Project Blue Book. In it he stated, "based on additional information submitted to our UFO investigation officer, Wright-Patterson AFB, Ohio, we have been unable to identify the object you observed on September 3, 1965." With that, the legend of the 'Incident at Exeter' was born.

My presentation went off without a hitch that evening and could not have done so without the three core members of the KRI Center, Andy Kitt, Valerie

Lofaso, and a gentleman by the name of Mike Stevens. His name is synonymous with experiencers in New Hampshire. Experiencers, as Mike calls them, are people from every walk of life who have had encounters, in some way, with the UFO phenomenon.

I first heard of Mike Stevens through various circles of ufology. His name would come up anytime the Exeter UFO Festival was mentioned (he's a fixture there, typically narrating the trolley rides) or when the Betty and Barney Hill case is discussed in earnest. We communicated online for a little while about various functions at the KRI Center. I met him in person in February of 2018.

It was a late Saturday afternoon when I parked my vehicle at the KRI Center. I got out of my car and walked toward the trunk when a tough looking brute with hair covering the identifiable areas of his face approached me with purpose. He exhaled cigarette smoke and stretched a hand in greeting toward me. He smiled and said, "Nomar, right? Mike Stevens, nice to meet you. Need any help?" I was about to unload a box of books; I don't remember who carried them in, but it was probably Mike.

We talked like old friends as he showed me an intriguing picture of a beam of light captured at a camp in Jackson, New Hampshire. His eyes lit up as he spoke about the picture, the center, his work, and the UFO phenomena in general. It's easy to like him. He's kind and well spoken, reserved, yet open if he trusts you. He's first to lend a helping hand and the last one to leave to make sure everything is taken care of. He has created various groups over the years to help people cope with aspects of the paranormal. His most fulfilling and sometimes harrowing is the

Granite Sky Services. There, he helps people through the trauma of extraterrestrial encounters and abduction experiences.

The help his services provide come in many forms. From personal and family support sessions to private and public experiencer group support. The *GraniteSky.org* website states, "Our personal one on one support sessions are ideal for a range of situations. For those who are just coming to terms with their experiences to those who have been dealing with it for years. Our family support sessions offer the same support as our private sessions. These experiences can affect families, either directly or through the actions and emotions of the experiencer. Our family support sessions are designed to help families pull together through these experiences."

Granite Sky Services also offers, "…two varieties of group support. A private group comprised of Granite Sky clients who have had sessions and a public group open to the general public who have had experiences. Group sharing allows for a wider variety of experiences and perspectives to be openly discussed."

Along with one-on-one, family, and group counseling, he also offers ongoing support and a unique service called "Breaking Through Support". "We believe that these experiences take time to understand. We are happy to offer ongoing support and case studies. Whether it's looking into past experiences or being there for you during ongoing experiences. It can be a difficult situation to let your family and friends know you have been struggling with extraterrestrial encounters. We are happy to assist and support you in letting them know."

Mike takes on most, if not all, of this work on his own. It's work that is important to him. It's more than just a passion; it's his life. He knows about the subject, he knows about the trauma, and he knows how life altering it can all be. He knows because he is an experiencer himself and this is his story.

As Above, So Blue Infant
(1979)

*O*ur Universe has fascinated scholars, philosophers, writers, poets, mothers, fathers, children and nearly every person from every walk of life throughout humanity's existence. Many have pontificated about our role within the Universe, how we fit in, and what the meaning of it could truly be. A well-known quote about the Universe is often attributed to Arthur C. Clark but is actually taken from an interview with Stanley Kubrick. In 1965, physicist and author Jeremy Bernstein wrote a piece for *The New Yorker's* "Talk of the Town" about Kubrick, who, at the time, was at the cusp of releasing his collaborative work with Arthur C. Clarke, *2001: A Space Odyssey*. During this interview, Kubrick was said to be quoting a writer, which many assumed to be Clarke, though never confirmed. Regardless of its origin, the quote is thought provoking and reads, "Two possibilities exist: Either we are alone in the Universe or we are not. Both are equally terrifying."

Fourteen years after that quote was spoken into the cosmos, Mike Stevens was born. He came into the world on January 20, 1979 at Wentworth Douglas Hospital in Dover, New Hampshire. His parents, Mick and Karen Stevens were thrilled.

1979 was a volatile year, cosmically speaking. In March of that year, the first extraterrestrial volcano was discovered. Linda Morabito was an astronomer with NASA's Jet Propulsion Laboratory who discovered volcanic activity on a moon of Jupiter called Io. While she performed analysis of images from Voyager 1, she detected a 170-mile-tall cloud off a limb of Io. Her discovery was the first in history to show volcanism off Earth. She made this finding on March 9, 1979. In August of that year, the first known celestial body collided with the Sun. A 1981 *New York Times* article reported, "A comet collided violently with the Sun two years ago, generating tremendous energy and scattering debris millions of miles across the solar system, scientists at the Naval Research Laboratory reported today. The event, recorded by satellite instruments, is the first known instance of a celestial body colliding with the Sun, said Dr. Donald J. Michels. It also marks the first time a comet has been discovered by a satellite. Dr.

Michels said the collision, which occurred Aug. 30, 1979, was recorded by an experiment called Solwind." While new discoveries and violent cosmic collisions were happening in space, a young Mike Stevens, not even a year old, suffered on Earth.

Around the time of the comet's collision with the sun, Mick's son was brought to a hospital due to an odd occurrence with the infant's skin. In an interview I conducted with Mike he said of the trauma, "I was drinking formula, I was fine as far as my parents knew, and then all of a sudden they noticed that I had turned blue. They rushed me down to the hospital and the doctor kind of blew them off. The doctor told them, 'There's nothing wrong with the kid, you're new parents, you're just overreacting.' My parents told me that they looked at each other and said, 'No! The kid is blue, something is wrong with him.' So, they went for a second opinion where another doctor said I was severely dehydrated. This confused my parents because I was drinking normally over the past few months and would have no reason to be dehydrated." Mike's parents had no other choice than to heed the doctor's recommendation and make sure that Mike was getting his fluids. After a few hours, his color returned to normal.

I researched causes for an infant's skin to turn blue and found some interesting information. According to *Medical News Today*, "Blue baby syndrome, also known as infant methemoglobinemia, is a condition where a baby's skin turns blue. This occurs due to a decreased amount of hemoglobin in the baby's blood. Hemoglobin is a blood protein that is responsible for carrying oxygen around the body and delivering it to the different cells and tissues. When the blood is unable to carry oxygen around the body, the baby turns blue (cyanotic). Blue baby syndrome is rare in industrialized countries, but it does occasionally occur in rural areas. Babies born in developing countries with poor water supply continue to be at risk for the condition." The last sentence of that quote is interesting as it does bring water into the equation, perhaps denoting the second doctor's opinion of dehydration being accurate or at least related. Upon further research, I found that the type of water that baby formula is mixed with could be a cause for the syndrome. *Medical News Today* reported, "The most common cause of blue baby syndrome is water contaminated with nitrates. After a baby drinks formula made with nitrate-rich water, the body converts the nitrates into nitrites. These nitrites bind to the hemoglobin in the body, forming methemoglobin, which is unable to carry oxygen. Nitrates are most common in drinking water in farming communities that use well water. This contamination is due to the use of fertilizers and manure. Infants younger than 3 months are at highest risk for blue baby syndrome, but it can also occur in other populations." Mike was born in rural New Hampshire and in a follow up conversation that we had about the incident, he told me that his parents lived in Somersworth during 1979. They did not have well water; their water supply was provided by the city. Does that mean that Somersworth's water supply did or did not contain nitrates in 1979? It's impossible to say at this point, however, when researching Somersworth water supply information from 2017, the report on their water quality stated, "We continually refine and advance water treatment techniques in response to new regulations and our duty to provide safe and clean water for our customers. This requires us to perform extensive water sample collection and analysis for many different waterborne substances including: pH, conductivity, Color, Turbidity, Coliform, Cryptosporidium, Total Organic Carbon; Disinfection Byproducts (TTHM/HAA5); Lead and Copper, Iron, Manganese, **Nitrates**; Volatile/Synthetic Organic and Inorganic Chemicals (VOC/ SOC/IOC); Alkalinity." The bolded text would indicate that the city actively and aggressively makes sure that their water supply is tested for nitrates and numerous other waterborne substances. The "nitrate section" from that same water quality report did state the town's nitrate levels are at an "ND" level which stands for "not detectable at testing limit". The report further stated, "Nitrate in drinking water at levels above 10ppm is a health risk for infants of less than six months of age. High nitrate levels in drinking water can cause blue baby syndrome. Nitrate levels may rise quickly for short periods of time because of rainfall or agricultural activity."

    Moving on from terrestrial causes for blue skinned infants, I also researched blue skinned beings reported in ufology and found the following information from the *Hybrids Rising* website, "The Blues or Extraterrestrials with blue skin remain a rather elusive and little understood race or species of Extraterrestrials interacting with Humans. Bona fide reports of beings with blue skin are somewhat difficult to come by. Most written accounts encompass ancient history and religion while much information on the Internet concerning different 'alien types,' especially concerning beings with blue skin, contains misinformation mixed with folklore and mythology." I've written about folklore in ufology before and besides the stories themselves, folklore has generated what is referred to as a "folk-belief". In the book, *Wonders in the Sky: Unexplained Aerial Objects from Antiquity to Modern Times*, Dr. David J. Hufford wrote, "This term was, and still is, generally reserved for beliefs that are at odds in some way with the official modern worldview." Much of ufology is still seen in this manner despite recent *New York Times* articles that depict the Pentagon's involvement in researching and investigating reports of UFOs. In my opinion, it is fair to denote that folk-belief could be swaying modern believers of alien life in a way that is non-scientific. The point here is to discuss the experiencer point of view. As Mike has often said, "People, not proof."

All sorts of people struggle with all sorts of mental ailments. I, myself, struggle with medically diagnosed anxiety and depression. During therapy sessions, my therapist genuinely listened to me and provided advice, coping skills, and recommendations. They were insightful, non-judgmental, and open to what I told them about myself, trigger points and my experiences. People like Mike Stevens, Budd Hopkins, and countless others have provided similar services to people suffering from extraterrestrial trauma. Because of the sensitive nature of these events and the scrutiny surrounding them, I did want to point out that it has been discussed and written about within the medical field. I previously covered this type of trauma in *Otherworldly Encounters*. In it I wrote, "Post Abduction Syndrome (PAS) is a concept which states that people who have experienced one or more alien abductions (especially as children) could develop a syndrome of anxiety induced stress, similar to PTSD. The abduction syndrome was first introduced in 1992 by Dr. David M. Jacobs, Budd Hopkins, and Dr. Ron Westrum in their report, *Unusual Personal Experiences: An Analysis of the Data from Three Major Surveys*. Registered Nurse, Rose Hargrove wrote a dissertation on PAS called, *Post Abduction Syndrome (PAS): Description of an Emerging Syndrome...*"

Is it within the realm of possibility that an alien/human hybrid could be a possible cause for blue skinned infants? The *Hybrids Rising* website provided some additional information and experiencer quotes that could infer that possibility: "According to Abductee-Experiencers, some of the Blues have light blue skin that glistens or shimmers when the light reflects off of their skin… The Blue beings, like all other beings Abductee-Experiencers are interacting with, have a typical humanoid appearance (one head, a torso, two arms and hands, and two legs and feet)." One of those blue beings, it has been reported, told an experiencer that, "I always have blue-gray skin when I incarnate into the Earth plane." Another experiencer reported, "I held a male child who had white/blond hair and pale blue skin. His skin was beautiful and glistened even in the dim light. This young boy was scared and was crying and told me he believed other ones were using him and would eventually kill him."

If we are to extrapolate meaning behind these two potential causes for an infant's skin to turn blue, I believe it would be fair to say that some readers may find the first cause (contaminated water) easy to believe and that the second cause (alien/human hybrids) harder to believe. To ask someone like Budd Hopkins, Mike Stevens, or even my former therapist, which cause would be easier for them to believe? They would probably listen with an open mind and get to the heart of the question; it's not about belief, it's about the person. In Mike's case, in 1979, two doctors were dismissive about Blue Baby Syndrome. The syndrome was first discovered in 1945 so, this wasn't a case of a newly discovered syndrome being overlooked by uniformed doctors. In my opinion, this was a case of two doctors not listening to their patient. Perhaps more could have been done to learn about Mike's situation, but the opportunity was sadly lost. If some tests were performed, maybe it would have been found that Mike has an RH negative blood type. For some researchers of ufology, that particular blood type may correlate to alien abduction. *Gaia.com* wrote, "In 1901, Austrian born Dr. Karl Landsteiner used a mix of Rhesus monkey and rabbit blood to determine agglutination, a clumping response in certain combinations of blood that led to the discovery of blood types A, B, O & AB and explained previous violent reactions and sometimes death from blood transfusions. This led to blood typing and higher success rates in transfusions. Twenty-nine years later, in 1930, furthering research on blood, Landsteiner repeated the procedure using human blood and rabbit blood. There he found a common factor between the Rhesus monkey blood and human blood in its clumping response, dubbing the factor as Rh positive – having the same factor as the Rhesus monkey. Approximately 85% of the human population is Rh positive, where blood cells contain the D antigen as it was called, a substance on surface of the red blood cell that triggers antibodies. Those without the Rh factor or D antigen, called Rh negative, comprise only 15% of the population." A large percentage of reported alien abductees have indicated that their blood type is RH negative. This is certainly relevant when discussing the trait similarities within blood types. According to *Gaia*, all blood types other than RH negative can be mapped through evolution. *Gaia* continued, "Rh-Positive shares the trait similarity with other species, specifically apes, the Rh-Positive bloodline can be mapped through time and evolution. Rh negative cannot. It has no similarities or earthly trace. So, where did Rh negative come from? Since the discovery of blood types over a hundred years ago, little else has been identified by science as to how our blood types originated and why they exist at all. However, in putting together the history of evidence and modern science, theorists believe the Rh-Negative blood type points to alien ancestors and the merging of two distinct DNAs."

  I personally do not subscribe to any of Gaia's services, nor do I use them often in research. I think the company is self-serving and delivers agenda ridden media to an already engaged audience that lacks serious research. So, why did I reference them here? As you'll see throughout the book, I attempt to use a balanced approach for resources. I'll present one side, then the other and ultimately, everything in this book is just a means to tell Mike's story. Also, as a side note and as of this writing, Mike has not had his blood type checked.

Sharing the "blue infant" story is not about proving or disproving extraterrestrial intervention. Instead, it is to remind us about the power of being heard. The vulnerability in which a survivor of trauma must withstand is complex and unique for the individual. I beg of us all to allow kindness and understanding to become an innate response.

Strange Invaders
(1983)

It could be said that one of Hollywood's most prolific years in movie production occurred in 1983. There were numerous sequel misfires such as *Psycho II*, *Jaws 3-D*, *Superman III*, and *Amityville 3-D*. Conversely, it was one of Hollywood's brightest moments with the release of *Star Wars: Return of the Jedi* and the discovery and embracement of Stephen King's brand of horror with the releases of *The Dead Zone*, *Cujo* and *Christine*. A lesser known sci-fi movie was released in September of 1983 called *Strange Invaders*. It did not perform well at the box office and was originally the second movie in a "Strange Trilogy" after its 1981 predecessor *Strange Behavior*. The concept was abandoned after *Strange Invaders,* but the movie spoke to numerous points in modern ufology. There were researchers from an organization called "The National Center for UFO Studies". For many current researchers in the field, this will harken back to J. Allen Hynek's "Center for UFO Studies" whose archives are still available to this day (cufos.org). A plot point in the movie is that of the Eisenhower Administration and how they may have entered into a secret, long-term treaty with representatives from another planet. Again, astute UFO researchers would be hard-pressed not to think of the reports of Eisenhower interrupting a Palm Springs vacation to meet with aliens. *Huffpost* reported, "The story about Eisenhower's close encounter of the very personal kind — where he reportedly met with Nordic-looking aliens — supposedly unfolded while the president was vacationing in Palm Springs, Calif., in February 1954. Per the Eisenhower Library in Abilene, Kansas, it was merely an emergency trip to the dentist. Whether you believe this story or not, an interesting related side-story reared its head in 2010. A retired New Hampshire state representative, Henry McElroy Jr., taped an intriguing video announcement in which he revealed seeing a secret briefing document intended for Eisenhower. This document, according to McElroy, contained information that aliens were in America and that Eisenhower could meet with them." For me personally, Huffpost is not my go-to information provider, but they did concisely marry the Eisenhower meetings with the McElory video. If nothing else, it sheds more light on New Hampshire's quiet stronghold on notable ufological events.

The First Encounter

Another notable event from 1983, only whispered about in certain UFO circles, is that of Mike Stevens. It was a late spring/early summer evening in South Hampton, New Hampshire. The sun was only hinting of its slow departure to the west when a young boy walked around a family function inside of his grandmother's home. Mike was four years old and recalled most of the event in scant memories until the unforgettable happened. In my sit-down with Mike, he talked at length about the incident that was unknowingly the catalyst for a lifetime of otherworldly encounters. He started by saying, "Off the dining room was a three-season sunporch that overlooked the back yard. As I walked by that, there was an immediate urge or calling to get outside." As I typed away on my laptop, I couldn't help but think of my own encounter at 4 years-old. I, too, felt the urge to look outside, though my urge was not sparked by a calling, but of lightning. I wrote about it extensively in a previous book and I felt it merited a mention as my perspective on Mike had grown to see him as a kindred spirit. Mike kept talking during my daydream and I was thankful that I was recording the interview on audio while my mind wandered and notes were missed. He continued, "I don't remember how I got outside but I found myself in the driveway." My mind wanders again now as I listen to the recording of Mike's testimony and write this portion of the book.

I'm immediately back in my driveway, a day before our interview was to commence. It's ten o'clock in the morning and my 2013 Ford Escape contains my luggage, a tote of food, and myself. The engine idles as I stare off into nothing. I'm thinking about my last meeting with Mike in Kennebunk, Maine. That was our first long form interview in February of 2019, and I was floored by the experiences he shared. I recorded that conversation as well, and I have referred to it numerous times, always wishing I had asked certain follow up questions. While many were eventually addressed in phone calls, texts, and messages on Facebook, his story is so intricate and complicated, a second longform conversation was warranted. We set up a meeting at his office in Newmarket, New Hampshire. At that time, the area, along with southern Maine, was just two days removed from the first major snowstorm of the winter season (12/3/2019) and was pounded with about a foot of snow. In my area, near Bar Harbor, Maine, we could still see grass, dirt, and tar. Definitely not typical. I shook off the thought, pressed the brake, pulled the gear shift into drive, and continued my research into Mike Stevens' story.

    Back in Mike's office, he continued to tell me about the encounter. "My cousin is out there as well, she's about six months older than I am, we're kinda just standing there. The next thing you know, we see the woods behind my grandmother's house light up with something like a bright red glow and as that's happening, we see a saucer-shaped craft emerge just above the tree line. From there, the craft floated its way across the lawn towards us. There used to be a big tree there and it parked itself, hovering, just to the side of my grandmother's house." I'm right in that moment with him, my mind no longer wandering. I can picture Mike and his cousin, small children, looking up at an aerial oddity, not necessarily scared but confused and curious. Earlier that day, Mike took me to the location of his grandmother's home. He shared a brief version of the encounter while we were there and I took some photographs of the landscape that are contained within this book. I looked up into the same sky that he had that early evening in 1983. In fact, we looked up together as he spoke and pointed to the area of the hovering craft. We shared an impromptu moment of silence at the weight of the situation before getting back into my car.

"It was 40 or 50 feet wide and the height was probably half that," Mike said after taking a sip of coffee.

"Ok," I said while completing a note in my laptop, "…it comes towards you, it's hovering now, how high?"

Mike estimated about 45 feet in the air and said at this point, he and his cousin have gotten a "good look" at the craft. He continued, "It's got that classic saucer shape to it and got what seems like a metal body hull, shiny, chrome-like. Around the middle there's a row of lights. They change color in a sequence as it strobes around the whole craft. It doesn't seem like individual bulbs; it almost seems more like fluid with how the colors change. It kept the same pattern for a while but then the pattern changed in intensity and speed. It started flashing faster and when that happened, an interior light came on within the craft."

I'm typing recklessly, trying to capture every detail; my mind is not on the audio recorder anymore.

I just know that I need to capture everything that he's saying. Mike has a way of speaking when he's comfortable; calm, passionate and captivating. I was drawn into his event, hanging on every word. He continued, "You could make out a row of windows above the lights around the center of the craft. Inside was kind of like a soft yellow light, like a car's interior bulb. Inside of that, you could see shadows of humanoid figures, you couldn't make out any details or anything." I pressed him on this and asked him if there was anything at all distinguishable that he could make out of the shadows. He thought for a moment and said, "All you could really see is like a shadow of head and shoulders. It wasn't really telling of anything." I then asked if he could, in any way, discern the height of the shadows that he observed. He recalled that the windows were approximately three to four feet high and he could see the shadow from its perceived waist/torso to just above the top of its head. The top of the window, he said, was essentially the top of the craft, and if we are to project human sensibilities in its construction, with most windows in our homes starting approximately at waist height, we could infer that the shadow humanoid was approximately five to six feet tall. Or, all of that is incorrect and we have no idea. Mike and I shared a laugh at that thought and then he said, "I couldn't see anything to tell if they were looking at us but I had this strong feeling we were being stared at. And not just… it's hard to explain, like something was watching us and I just knew the situation was going to turn bad. It was like this internal instinct like primal fear at that moment. Something was wrong."

That entire statement gave me goosebumps. I looked up from my laptop when he said that and my chest got that fluttering feeling, all of which I kept to myself. "The intensity of that fear lasted maybe around thirty seconds," Mike added, "and that was where my standing memory had a blank." I asked him to explain what he meant by that. He could only articulate that after that intense feeling of fear, the craft had moved, in an instant, to just above a telephone pole at the edge of his grandmother's property. I asked how fast it had moved there from its previous location and he could only disjointedly explain that there was like a skip in time or perhaps, missing time. He and his cousin had instantly moved a few feet over to the side of where they had been standing previously and the craft had moved to above the telephone pole, almost like a bad edit in a sci-fi b-movie.

I looked at him inquisitively and asked, "What do you think happened during the time that you can't remember, and do you know how much time had passed?" He swallowed another sip of coffee and said, "I always felt there was more. It didn't make sense that it was here and then it was there." He gestured with his hand; pointing at one location of the ceiling, then to another. He continued, "There had to be time in the middle but I don't know what it was." I asked him if he thought that missing middle piece could have been abduction. He looked at me for a long moment, his eyes emoting a lifetime of encounters, confusion and unanswered questions. "I don't know," he eventually said. It was a simple answer but subliminally complex. I felt a lot within that moment and response. I thought, "Mike is brave." Brave because he raised a daughter, held jobs, and maintained friendships and relationships after surviving that encounter. He even devoted himself to helping others understand their own I-don't-knows. And, it was also sad. Sad because he still doesn't know what happened to him. Sad because there are those who will never believe him; this was just the beginning and he had no idea. I wrote the following note in that moment of the interview as, "Mike's eyes are telling me everything and I just want to hug him." I didn't and regret it but Mike wouldn't want me to. Instead, I asked him what happened next. "It hovered over the telephone pole for a little bit. It almost seemed like it was making sure everything was ok." He smirked at the thought and continued with, "It then just went straight up, as quick as can be and disappeared. It almost seemed like it got sucked up into somewhere." I asked him if there was any sound emanating from the craft and also asked if the sound in the environment around them seemed different. "There was no sound from the craft," he said. "I don't know if my age played into it at all, but everything just kinda shut off. All I was focused on was the craft."

    That was the entirety of the encounter as he remembered it. He thought about the experience for some time after but did not talk about it often with his cousin. When it *was* brought up, Mike said, "It was just surface conversations, we didn't really discuss it. It wasn't until I was older when I called her to talk about it." I asked him what the catalyst was for the phone call. He said that it was due to a hypnosis session that he had.

Hypnotic Regression

In 2010, Mike was part of a paranormal investigation team and visited the home of a hypnotist who was having, as Mike put it, "a spiritual/ghost problem." The medium on Mike's team, who was in charge of cleansing the property, had agreed to a trading of services with the hypnotist. The medium offered a full cleansing and the hypnotist offered all members of the investigation team past life regression sessions. When the team showed up for their sessions, Mike was told by the hypnotist that he didn't need a regression. What he needed instead was to remember what happened during a childhood encounter. Mike was startled by the revelation and was open to the hypnosis process. "I wasn't quite expecting it," Mike said. "I wasn't going in there to relive that at that moment, ya know? But I was open to it." Mike sat in the chair and was given a verbal set of instructions to place him under hypnosis. The following is a partial transcript of that session and provides insight into the possibility of abduction.

Hypnotist – "What else is happening? Just let the scene move forward."

Mike – "There's a… there's… things are not… there's people in it."

Hypnotist – "Can you describe them?"

Mike – "No, it's just shadowy, it's outliney, there's… it's like an interior light in a car or something that went on."

Hypnotist – "Ok. So, did perhaps a door open or

hatch open?

Mike – "Not that I see."

Hypnotist – "Ok. What are these creatures doing? These people, these beings. They moving towards you? Or?"

Mike – "No, they're still in the thing. It's almost… they're… it's a lot of… it feels like staring. I can't see faces but it's… it's very… being watched… almost… it's more than being watched. They feel like they're in you."

Hypnotist – "Ok. It's still you and your cousin?"

Mike – "I don't know. I don't see her anymore."

Hypnotist – "Ok. Detach yourself from any discomfort, just describe what you're seeing; what you're experiencing. Detach yourself from any sense of fear. You're simply telling a story. So, you have this sense of them watching you and actually perhaps being inside of you. And now what?"

Mike – "I don't think they're physically inside me."

Hypnotist – "Right."

Mike – "I don't know."

Hypnotist – "So, what happens next?"

Mike – "I'm just kinda stuck at that image. But I can start to vaguely hear a hum now."

Hypnotist – "Ok. So, the craft is hovering overhead. You have a sense of being watched but more than just being watched. You can hear a hum. And what happens next?"

Mike – "The lights… the lights change."

Hypnotist – "How do they change? The color, the brightness?"

Mike – "The umm… the light bar. It's… it's not

a single color anymore… its umm, multicolored now."

Hypnotist – "Ok, any separate colors?"

Mike – "Umm… They vary but it's more of the reddish range of colors. Reds to oranges to yellows."

Hypnotist – "Ok. What else is happening? The lights have changed."

Mike – "They almost strobe or stroll. Not so much flashing. It almost seems like the color sequence rolls in a pattern."

Hypnotist – "Ok. And you're still in the driveway?"

Mike – "Yeah."

Hypnotist – "Ok. And then what happens? Just let the story tell itself."

LONG PAUSE

Mike – "I… I'm, alright… I'm not in the driveway. I don't… I see almost… It's not a conveyer belt but it almost looks like a grated steel conveyer belt but not like chains, like slats."

Hypnotist – "Similar to an escalator perhaps?"

Mike – "Yeah. But almost… more like, more like siding or.... It's not like… it rolls smoother, it's not like chainy or clicky."

Hypnotist – "Ok. What are you sensing? Or, is someone coming down from the craft, or are you moving up towards the craft?"

Mike – "I think I'm in it."

Hypnotist – "You're in the craft now?"

Mike – "I think. I seem to be in some type of doorway type thing, I don't know how I got to that point."

Hypnotist – "Ok, just tell me what you see, what

you hear, what you feel."

Mike – "I feel physically cold but it's… I can't really make out a lot of shapes or details but it's very… not bright but well lit. Very white soft light not blinding but…"

Hypnotist – "Have you had a better glimpse of the people?"

Mike – "No."

Hypnotist – "Ok."

Mike – "I feel like there's things around, but I don't… I don't see anybody."

Hypnotist – "When you say things you mean beings?"

Mike – "Yes."

Hypnotist – "Ok. So, you're standing essentially at the doorway?"

Mike – "Yeah. I think I'm passed that. I feel… I don't know if it's a room or the whole thing but I feel centered in it."

Hypnotist – "Ok. You're standing?"

Mike – "Yes."

Hypnotist – "Do you sense any type of communication from these beings?"

Mike – "Not at this point. It's more… just kind of a… being dumbfounded."

Hypnotist – "Ok."

Mike – "There's… dumb, yeah, dumbfounded maybe a little disbelief like what's going on? But it's not… I don't feel… I don't feel fear.

Hypnotist – "Ok. Then what do you experience next?"

Mike – "I see one. He's… tall. I don't… I don't know if he's tall-tall, or if I'm just short."

Hypnotist – "Ok. Describe the features."

Mike – "I only caught a quick glimpse and I didn't really see his face. It… he moved passed me and almost hunched when he walked. He… he… his… wherever is, that wouldn't have been his normal thing, I don't think. It… to his physical attributes… it… he looked hunched, not like it would be comfortable to be like that all the time."

Hypnotist – "Ok. Was the form human like? Arms, legs, torso, head?"

Mike – "Yeah. Legs, I didn't really catch, it was more, assuming he must have had them, but it was more… hips up. The arm, if you looked at a human arm, it seemed like the wrist was longer from like where your wrist should be. Instead of just going to a hand it almost seemed like another short piece of forearm there. Or it could have been the way he held it. He looked crunched when he came through."

Hypnotist – "Mmhmm. Was it clothed?"

Mike – "I… I don't think so."

Hypnotist – "Ok. How did it's covering or skin appear?"

Mike – "Not… not wet. Not like drippy wet. But almost a shine to it, kinda, almost."

Hypnotist – "Was there a color to it?"

Mike – "Olive, olivey drab to a brownish type gray."

Hypnotist – "Very good, very good. What else do you perceive or see or hear?"

Mike – "The hum is pretty constant and the light is just engulfing. It's hard to make much out of the light. You can see in it, but it's not like having a light in your face."

Hypnotist – "Ok. And you're still standing in the center?"

Mike – "No."

Hypnotist – "Where are you now?"

Mike – "I'm lying down, or I'm floating. I'm not vertical."

Hypnotist – "So, you are horizontal?"

Mike – "Yeah."

Hypnotist – "Are you on a table or a bed of some sort or just hovering?"

Mike – "I don't know. It's… I don't feel anything under me. It's comfortable."

Hypnotist – "Ok. Do you notice any sensations around your body?"

Mike – "There's movement by my feet… but it's… I think there's things down there walking past but I can't see them."

Hypnotist – "Ok. Do you get any sense at all of how many of them there might be?"

Mike – "I would say at least three from earlier when I was still outside and you could still see shadows."

Hypnotist – "Ok. Do you get a sense of what they want?"

Mike – "It almost… I don't know… they want… it's almost… it was supposed, more of a feeling it was supposed to happen. It's almost… they're not celebrating me but it's almost like a birthday party there for me. But I don't know what they want."

Hypnotist – "So, they are there specifically for you."

Mike – "Yeah."

Hypnotist – "This was not a chance happening?"

Mike – "No."

Hypnotist – "It was not random?"

Mike – "No."

Hypnotist – "Is this the first time you ever experienced this? At around age three?"

Mike – "It's the first time I consciously remembered but it's not feeling like that now."

Hypnotist – "Some things are feeling a little familiar?"

Mike – "Yeah."

Hypnotist – "Again, do you get any sense of them communicating with you on any level? Telepathically, orally, auditorily."

Mike – "No, but… there's… they are trying to make me comfortable. Nobody said it, I just feel it."

Hypnotist – "Ok. What else is happening? You're lying there, you feel comfortable. You feel welcomed. You have a sense that this is supposed to be. So, what else can you tell me about this encounter?"

Mike – "It's kinda just like… going, it's a checkup, it's like a checkup, like at the doctors. Not so much the medical instrument. I don't see any of that I just… the feeling is a checkup."

Hypnotist – "Do you sense that they are somehow scanning you physically?"

Mike – "I couldn't tell ya at this point. I don't see it. More like a perception."

Hypnotist – "Do you have any indication that they have implanted anything in you? Helping them find you?"

Mike – "I don't know. Everything seems very… it's not in my face. Everything seems to be happening away from my eyes and everything's lower by my feet. I don't think they are actually touching my feet. The commotion of the hustle and bustle is at my feet and… I… I don't see it, but my perception is… maybe there is… maybe one at each side, shoulder area, maybe another by my head but I don't if… I think they're more of a distraction. I… it feels like whatever is going on is by my feet."

Hypnotist – "What else can you tell me about this experience? This encounter."

LONG PAUSE

Mike – "The commotion at my feet isn't… isn't for me."

Hypnotist – "Any idea who it's for?"

Mike – "My cousin."

Hypnotist – "It's your cousin, ok. And what's happening with her?"

Mike – "I don't know, I kinda just snapped out of it."

END OF SESSION

With all of those memories now on the surface, Mike placed a phone call to his cousin to discuss their mutual encounter in full; he wanted to know exactly what she remembered. "I said, tell me what you remember and then I'll tell you what I remember. She started telling me that we're sitting on my grandmother's porch playing and that a red light appeared in the sky. It was, for lack of a better term, dancing around in the sky. She said it really seemed like it was putting on a show for us. It felt like it was there for us to see and doing what it had to do to be noticed. She said it softly went out, kinda like how it came in." Mike asked if she remembered how old they were when this occurred. She told him they were around 3 or 4 years-old. Mike disagreed and thought that was a different encounter and that it happened when they were around 10 years-old. Despite that, he told her everything that he remembered, he said, "She didn't remember any of that. She didn't disbelieve me or anything, but she didn't remember." Mike said of his cousin, "She became very open psychically. She began talking to relatives who had passed away and was able to describe them accurately to other family members." Mike also said that it seemed as though she continued having extraterrestrial encounters separately from Mike. "She said she experienced observing the Statue of Liberty from above even though she had never been in a plane going over it before." This implied to Mike that abductions may have been on-going for her. I asked him if he still talks to her about it; he does not.

Mike's cousin did not return my messages about discussing the incident.

Betty and Barney and Beyond

Mike's experience in 1983 may seem inconceivable to those unfamiliar with the extraterrestrial phenomena. When the passive consumer of strange happenings finds themselves engrossed in an alien narrative, it's been my experience that they are most likely consuming stories known more at a national level. Stories such as Area 51, the Roswell UFO Crash and recent news articles about "tic tac" UFOs, Tom DeLonge and Pentagon UFO programs. When you look just a little below the surface, copious amounts of stories emerge. The kind that make you think something more may be happening than we all realize. When reading accounts, such as the Exeter Incident, that include testimony from police officers and a government investigation into the incident, the word "inconceivable" reconstructs to "conceivable". New Hampshire has been host to many otherworldly events throughout the years; the following accounts are a brief overview of the Granite State's contributions to UFO lore.

Betty and Barney Hill Abduction

A social worker and a postal employee walk into a boarding house…. While this could lend itself to a variant of the old "bar joke", it is actually how Betty Barrett met Barney Hill. In the *Ultimate Book of Jokes* by author Scott McNeely, the first bar joke was published in 1952. It wasn't until four years later, in 1956, when Barney and Betty met. Their unexpected kinship turned into a relationship and they were married four years after that, in 1960. Due to employment commitments, the beginning of their marriage was essentially a long-distance union. Barney worked and resided in Philadelphia while Betty worked and lived in Portsmouth, New Hampshire. Almost a year later, Barney was able to transfer to a postal service job in Boston, allowing him and Betty to live together in Portsmouth. Once they were settled and living together, they finally began talking about taking the long-overdue honeymoon they'd had to delay while living apart. In September of 1961, Barney surprised Betty with time off from his new job and it was decided that they would drive to Niagara Falls the next day. Since it was a spur of the moment trip, there wasn't much time to plan and prepare and they ended up not having as much spending money as they had hoped. Despite this, they were up for an adventure and decided to pack food and, if need be, sleep in the car for a night or so.

They started their trip on Sunday, September 17, slowly making their way to Niagara Falls, then onto Toronto, and eventually Montreal. On Tuesday, September 19, they decided to get a hotel room in Montreal to enjoy the city's night spots and entertainment. Barney got lost while driving around Montreal and they had trouble locating a hotel room. There was also a tropical storm headed toward the east coast and they knew it would slow their return home and back to their jobs so instead of continuing to search for a room in the outskirts of Montreal, they decided to start their long trek back to New Hampshire. They knew they would have to drive into the early morning hours but, if they were careful and took their time, they would eventually reach their home early on Wednesday, September 20.

A little before 11pm, the Hills were south of Lancaster, New Hampshire. That was when Betty observed a bright point of light that moved uncharacteristically around the night sky. She brought it to Barney's attention but he was concentrated on the drive and was dismissive of the light. Betty eventually reasoned that it was a shooting star and looked away. Not long after, the light grew larger and brighter which caught Betty's attention. She again brought it to Barney's attention and was insistent that they pull over to observe it through binoculars. Barney agreed and stopped at a picnic area near Twin Mountain. Betty looked at the light through their binoculars and told her husband that it might be some sort of craft, maybe a UFO. Barney took a look and thought that it was probably just an airplane. As he continued to watch, the craft descended bizarrely and in their direction. This startled the Hills and they jumped into their car and drove off toward Franconia Notch.

As they drove, they continued to observe the craft and reported that it passed above a restaurant and Cannon Mountain. It went out of site for a moment and reemerged near the Old Man of the Mountain. The craft was so low at this point that Betty observed it rotating and estimated its diameter at 60-80 feet. They kept watch as it seemingly tailed them until it descended quickly toward their vehicle near the Indian Head area. Barney was dumbfounded and slammed on the brakes. They came to a stop in the middle of the road as the craft hovered low overhead. Out of curiosity, Barney stepped out of the vehicle and looked at the craft through the binoculars again. His eyes widened in terror when he observed a dozen or so humanoid figures all standing at the craft's bank of windows, staring at the Hills. In the book *Captured! The Betty and Barney Hill UFO Experience*, Stanton Friedman and Kathleen Marden wrote, "Lifting his binoculars to his eyes, Barney spied a group of humanoid figures moving about with the precision of German officers. As the craft tilted downward and began to descend toward him, one of the strange creatures that remained at the window communicated a frightening message. Barney had the immediate impression that he was in danger of being plucked from the field. Overcome with fear, and with all the courage he could muster, he tore the binoculars from his face and raced back to the car. Breathless, trembling, and in near hysterics, he told Betty that they needed to get out of there or they were going to be captured."

As they drove, Betty and Barney began feeling an odd buzzing sensation and could actually hear buzzing all around them and throughout their vehicle before it finally faded away. They didn't say much to each other during this time; the only goal was to get as far away from the craft as possible. After a while, the buzzing started again, and their thoughts became manic and then their minds dazed. They had unexplained memories of some sort of check point or road block, but none of it made sense. As their thoughts cleared, they realized they were getting closer to their destination and figured they'd arrive home around 3 o'clock in the morning. As they reached Portsmouth, day broke and their confusion returned; unable to understand how more time passed than was possible, they arrived home about two hours later than predicted.

Once home, Betty had the urge to keep their luggage by the back door, not wanting it in their home more than necessary. They reported that both of their watches stopped working and the strap on their binoculars was broken but neither had an explanation for its damage. Barney's shoes, previously free from scuffs, were now scraped and marked for unknown reasons. He also said that he felt an unexplained need to examine his genitals though ultimately found nothing out of the ordinary. Exhausted from their ordeal, they slept for a while. Once awake, Betty observed that her dress was damaged and that it had an odd, pink substance on it. They also found odd circle markings on the trunk of their car. Decades later, Marden unearthed some writings in a diary of Betty's and found one that chronicled their arrival home that morning in 1961. She wrote, "We entered our home, turned on the lights, and went over to the window and looked skyward. We stood there for several minutes. Then, Barney said, 'This is the most amazing thing that ever happened to me.' We both wondered if 'they' would come back. We felt very calm, peaceful, relaxed. We sat at the kitchen table, looked at each other, shook our heads in puzzlement, and asked each other, 'Do you believe what happened?' We agreed that it was unbelievable, but it had really happened. We would return to the window and look skyward."

Not long after returning home, Betty called her sister Janet and shared hers and Barney's experience. Janet had witnessed a UFO in the 1950s and Betty figured she would be non-judgmental of their harrowing encounter. After their conversation, the story ran rampant through the extended family, all never doubting the Hills. Some even suggested contacting Pease Air Force Base and using a compass to experiment with potential readings their vehicle might be giving off. Another writing of Betty's read, "I took the compass and went out to the car. Barney refused to go, saying that he was trying to forget what happened. It was still raining but I could see my car clearly under the street light in front of my home. I walked around it, holding the compass and not knowing what I was looking for. When I came to the trunk area, I saw many highly polished spots, about the size of a half dollar or silver dollar. The car was wet from the rain but these spots were clearly showing. I wondered what they were. I placed the compass over them, and it began spinning and spinning. I thought that it must be the way I was balancing the compass, so I placed it on the car and took my hand away. The compass was really spinning and continued to do this. As I was watching this, I was filled with an unexplained feeling of absolute terror. I was standing there in the rain, under the street light, and telling myself, 'Don't scream, keep calm, and don't be afraid, everything is alright.'"

On September 21, an apprehensive Betty called Pease Air Force Base to report their encounter. She did not tell them everything that happened but what she did share was enough to warrant a callback the next day from a Major Paul W. Henderson who sought more information on the encounter. Major Henderson filed a report on September 26 and ultimately determined that they merely misidentified the planet Jupiter. Betty, not pleased with the outcome of the report, wrote a letter to retired Marine Corps Major Donald E. Keyhoe, who was then head of the National Investigations Committee of Aerial Phenomena (NICAP). She related the entirety of their encounter, leaving nothing out and also shared that she and Barney were open to the idea of going under hypnosis to help them remember more of what happened. Eventually, a member of NICAP, Walter Webb, responded to the Hills and interviewed them extensively. The Hills were pleased to know that Webb believed them wholeheartedly.

Not long after their initial encounter, Betty had a series of dreams which seemingly detailed the goings-on of their missing time in elaborate detail. They were intense dreams of becoming apprehended by human-like soldiers and taken aboard a craft. She and Barney were separated, and Betty was subjected to a series of odd medical tests; she knew Barney was experiencing the same. Betty shared her dreams with Barney but he feared their implications and did not want to hear any more about them. As the years went by, the Hills shared their encounter with more people and even spoke publicly a few times around New Hampshire and Massachusetts. By happenstance, they met Ben Swett, a Captain from the Air Force who had a personal interest in hypnosis. After the Hills shared their encounter with him, they spoke of their consideration of hypnosis to help them not only recall the encounter but also to cope with the fallout. Barney especially was suffering and seeing a psychiatrist as a result. Swett recommended that Barney speak to his doctor so they could recommend a professional. They did just that, and on January 4, 1964, a Dr. Benjamin Simon began hypnosis sessions on the Hills, eventually ending in June of that same year. Through those sessions much was learned of the missing time the Hills had in 1961.

During Barney's sessions he recalled the non-human figures and was so frightened by them that he kept his eyes closed for most of his abduction experience. Barney also recalled that his binocular strap broke when he ran from the craft and back to his car. He remembered he and Betty fleeing the UFO but felt compelled to pull onto a dirt road where he witnessed six men standing. The car stopped moving on its own and was approached by the men on the road. When the men, or beings, stared into his eyes, he felt a mesmerizing effect and was very much afraid of their eyes. He recalled being taken to a room by three of the beings and told to lay on an examination table. Since Barney kept his eyes closed for most of the exam, those parts of his sessions are not as detailed as Betty's. He did remember hearing them communicate with one another in a language he did not understand. He also said that when they communicated with him, while in English, no words were spoken; instead, he heard it in his mind (this occurred with Betty, as well). He finally remembered being returned to their vehicle feeling heavily drugged or dazed.

Betty's memories during her sessions were quite similar to some dreams she had, but there were a few differences. The most dramatic pieces emerged in the form of a book and a star map. In one of her sessions, Betty spoke of a "leader" that she communicated with after her examination. The following excerpt is from John G. Fuller's book, *The Interrupted Journey*: "I felt, I was grateful to meet him because he stopped my pain, and now I wasn't afraid at all. And so, I started talking with the leader. And I said to him that this had been quite the experience. It was unbelievable. That no one would ever, ever believe me. And that most people didn't know he was alive. And that what I needed was some proof that this had really happened. So he laughed, and he said what kind of proof did I want? What would I like? And I said, well, if he could give me something to take back with me then people would believe it. And so he told me to look around, and maybe I could find something I would like to take. And I did–and there wasn't much around–but on the cabinet there was a book, a fairly big book." The leader asked Betty to look through the book, to see if she could understand any of it; she didn't, but still wanted it. Eventually he agreed and this delighted Betty. Toward the end of their abduction, the leader took the book away from Betty. She was upset and resistant. The leader explained that his colleagues, the other occupants of the craft, did not want her to take it and that she had to relinquish it, so she gave in.

In regards to the map, she revealed under hypnosis that the "leader" showed her a star map. From Fuller's book: "Betty Hill described a map she was shown 'by the leader aboard the ship.' Later, she sketched it. She said she was told that the heavy lines marked regular trade routes, and the broken lines recorded various space expeditions." The map was later used by Marjorie Fish, a school teacher and a Mensa member. From Friedman and Marden's *Captured!:* "Fish informed Betty that she had developed an interest in attempting to identify the astronomical location of the stars on the map that she was allegedly shown during her abduction. This gave Fish the chance to verify scientifically whether or not the star cluster Betty drew represented a real set of stars, suitable for planets, that could have developed life." Over a period of time, Fish was able to corollate data that, "seemed to substantiate the validity of Betty's star map."

Betty and Barney Hill's abduction has been

covered multiple times and in multiple mediums. From television and movies to books, magazine articles, and podcasts. To get the entirety of their encounter in varying degrees of detail I recommend the following:

- Books
  The Interrupted Journey by John G. Fuller
  Captured! The Betty and Barney Hill UFO Experience by Stanton Friedman and Kathleen Marden

- TV Movie
  The UFO Incident – Directed by Richard Colla, Universal Studios

- Web Series
  Rogue Mysteries – Directed by Bill Brock, Rogue Paramedia, Amazon Prime

- Website
  Kathleen-Marden.com

MADAR and the Kids

Another New Hampshire resident synonymous with the Exeter UFO Festival is research historian and freelance journalist, Dean Merchant. In fact, he and his wife Pamela are the founders of the festival and have dedicated themselves to providing a balanced event that appeals to both serious researchers of the phenomena and to the families of the community. In a 2015 article for *New Hampshire Magazine* writer Michael Berry wrote of Merchant, "He's accumulated quite a few stories, but ironically has never seen a definitive UFO himself. But he's seen and heard enough to construct theories about why the area in and around Exeter is such a hot spot for extraterrestrial visitations. 'They seem to be very curious about our use of nuclear things,' says Merchant. And between Seabrook's nuclear power station, the Portsmouth Naval Shipyard (which repairs nuclear subs) and the presence of the 509th Bomb Wing at Pease, Exeter is surrounded by 'nuclear things.' The 509th is a particularly intriguing factor to Merchant, since it made history on August 6, 1945, when the 509th's B-29 'Enola Gay' dropped the first atomic bomb on Hiroshima. Later, they were moved to an obscure air base in an even more obscure New Mexico town named Roswell. Then in 1958, the 509th relocated its planes and personnel to Pease Air Force Base within view of the open fields of Exeter."

Merchant, in my opinion, has an intriguing theory on the Hill case and how it could be connected to the incidents at Exeter and Roswell. Beyond that, he shared some intriguing stories in an article he wrote for *SeacoastOnline.com* called, "Close Encounters of the Second Kind in Stratham". In it, he related a UFO sighting near a gravel pit. He wrote, "On a wintry eve in 1971, three Stratham lads fired up their racing snow machines and departed from one of the youth's Stratham Heights Road homes." The kids were having fun riding through fields, enjoying the night and each other. As they rode a trail that would eventually lead them to Bunker Hill Avenue, they witnessed something none of them would soon forget. Merchant continued, "…as they reached the vicinity of the old Sanderson Gravel Pit, looming just above and nearly touching a high-power electrical line was the catalyst to heart-pounding, primal fear -- a UFO. Fleeing the apparition, the youthful trio turned and at full throttle retreated to the safety of the Heights Road home." The boys told their parents of the encounter and were so taken aback by their genuine fear, they had no choice but to believe them. In a somewhat otherworldly twist, a member of NICAP arrived to interview the friends. Merchant shared of the bizarre encounter, "Arriving soon at their door was John Oswald, a NICAP UFO investigator of local renown. Both parents remember the interview with Oswald as being eerie. 'He seemed to know what we would say before we spoke, as if he already knew what was in our minds,' they said. The boys were so uncomfortable they fled the house and interviewer as soon as possible. Dad recalls Investigator Oswald telling them about sensors that his people had set up in New Hampshire, all of which, he said, were triggered off at the precise time of the boys' encounter." In fairness to NICAP, colleagues were supportive of Oswald and deemed him an honest and hardworking researcher and hadn't meant to scare the boys. Now, the interesting piece to this story is of those "sensors" that Oswald mentioned. According to a NICAP archives report, a system was put into place around the Exeter area by Oswald. The report stated, "…during a 20-month period near Exeter, N.H. Oswald, intrigued by numerous sightings reported around Exeter during 1965-66, set out in late 1970 to establish and monitor a 'UFO detector' network surrounding this famous New England town. The timing for the experiment, Nov. 1970 through Sept. 1972, proved excellent, according to Oswald, who noted in a report to NICAP 'that significant UFO activity occurred within the test area during the period covered.'"

The system that Oswald referred to is called MADAR and is still in operation around the United States and over a dozen countries. According to the MADAR website (hosted by NICAP archives), "MADAR (Multiple Anomaly Detection & Automatic Recording), was designed by Lewis G. Blevins & Francis L. Ridge in 1960." As late as November 2019 the MADAR section of the NICAP website stated, "The MADAR Project has 93 MADAR sites or 'nodes' as they are called, located in the United States and several foreign countries. It is hoped that by end of this year there will be 100 such sites betraying the presence of UAPs. With the new Command Center located at Newburgh, Indiana, even the older MADAR-II system has been re-established. The MADAR Project is continuously delving into the unknown with the latest in technology." During Oswald's use of the equipment in the 1970s, NICAP reported, "…106 instances which are included in the Group 3 or Category 3 list of UFOs apparently producing 'electromagnetic effects'. E-M Effects are those which disrupt electrical circuits, cause engine failure in automobiles, produce radio interference, etc."

Unfortunately for Oswald, the sensors were not as successful as previously thought. He found that the sensors tended to be too sensitive and reported, "When I started building the detector network in New

Hampshire, I did not think that the instruments were sensitive enough to detect sunspot-related geomagnetic storms." And added, "Although it would appear that UFO's may have been detected on two occasions and that it is actually not possible to say that some other detector alarms were not caused by UFO's, it is clear that most of the hundreds of detector alarms recorded were caused by geomagnetic storm activity." Despite the sensor sensitivity issues, Oswald did have two concrete readings that coincided with witness encounters. The first being the boys from the gravel pit and the other, according to Oswald's report, occurred on, "Nov. 23, 1971, at 1:55 a.m., a large, fast-moving oval white light was observed by a single witness."

Other sightings in the area from the same timeframe were also written about in Merchant's *Seacoastonline.com* article. He wrote, "A few years after the incident, and just up the road, another group of Stratham youngsters experienced their own close encounter of a second kind." Five children were out sledding in an area called "the old hollow". Mike Stevens took me to this area, and I was able to photograph some of the landscape and sledding hill that Merchant refers to in the article. He continued, "Late on a snowy afternoon Tim Perry, a rough and tumble 10 year old, his sister and three chums were enjoying some fast sledding on the icy hill, when a bright, glaring aerial craft with white, green and red lights alternately flashing, descended onto the field across the road where Bob Wiggin Sr. planted his potatoes. 'It was late afternoon -- just getting dark,' says Perry. 'We saw a big light all of a sudden. It came out of nowhere, almost noiseless.' The kids, terrified like the three boys from the gravel pit, ran home and told their parents what they witnessed. They described the UFO as, 'roundish or slightly footballish...' The incident did not last long for the children as Perry explained, 'It stayed on the ground for maybe 10 seconds, went up slow, then phoom, it was gone..." Perry remembered that an investigator visited their home the next day and interviewed him and his sister separately, Merchant wrote in his article, "Tim recalls that he and his sister were interviewed separately. 'I was in the family kitchen,' he says. 'I remember his dark blue pants and light blue shirt, and being apprehensive as a boy would be if answering questions to a policeman.' Perry says the craft had melted a circular formation in the snowy field, about 50 feet in diameter and marked with weird patterns. He remembers three or four cars at the site and pictures and soil samples being taken. The next day it snowed and the physical tracings were buried beneath a white blanket. Today, as an engineer, husband and dad Perry can analytically ponder his childhood experience, but his mental parameters remain open to unknown explanations to what he saw decades ago."

The skies above Exeter and surrounding areas during the 1970s seemed to have harbored something that witnesses could not identify. The following stories would indicate that may still be true.

Recent Notable Reports

October 5, 2014 – The Everett Turnpike, which runs 44 miles from Concord, New Hampshire to the border of Massachusetts, was the scene of numerous witness reports of a "boomerang" shaped craft floating in the sky above Nashua. The website *Patch.com* reported, "…on late Sunday night while driving on the Everett Turnpike. The 'unidentified flying object' was described as having three bright lights with two smaller yellowish lights on the bottom, and appears to be similar to other triangle, boomerang objects that have been reported all around the nation during the last few years. The person reporting the incident stated that after picking up their son, they were driving north on the Everett Turnpike and saw 'what looked like an unusually bright star' in the distance. About a mile up the road, as they got closer to the object, they saw the bright white lights. Everyone in the vehicle saw the object, the article stated. 'There were no other identifying colored lights like our aircraft is required to have,' the writer reported. 'As we were nearing our exit, we could see it right over us through the moonroof heading west at slow but silent speed, and out of view over trees and buildings.'"

A few days after the *Patch.com* story came out, other witnesses came forward from other New Hampshire towns along the turnpike. Those places included, Manchester, Keene, Amherst, and Milford. In November of 2014, *Patch.com* wrote another story about more sightings over the Concord area (approximately 44 miles from Nashua, heading north). Staff writer for the news site, Tony Schinella, wrote, "…others have come forward saying they saw a similar object over the capital region the same week that the Nashua object was seen. According to a recent article on The Huffington Post, Ben Speigel, a Concord teen, took shots in the night sky of the North End on Oct. 5, of a bright orb in the sky about an hour before the Bowe family reported their sighting. Speigel said that a helicopter seemed to be following the orb. The orb, he said, was zigzagging back and forth across the sky. He took a picture on his iPod and then realized it was triangle shaped. About a week later, Brad-Leah Seigars, a reader from Boscawen, shot a photo around 2:30 p.m. on Oct. 11, of the orb flying over Boscawen, and submitted the picture to Concord NH Patch. The picture was taken above the Smoke Shack, a local BBQ joint, on King Street. It's unknown, at this time, what people were seeing in the skies. Mark Podell of the Mutual UFO Network thinks they could be advanced government aircraft. Bowe's not so sure, telling the Huffington Post, 'I think it was extraterrestrial, in my personal opinion. From what I witnessed, I've never seen a craft that could do that – being that big – float by without falling out of the sky and not making a sound. It wasn't a blimp or a drone.'" The striking photographs can be viewed by conducting a *Google* image search with the term, "Craft Was Seen in Concord, Boscawen Patch New Hampshire".

Sept. 21, 2015 – The following year, more witnesses came forward following a sighting above a mall in Concord. Schinella, once again, wrote the following account for *Patch*.com, "Mike Pittaro posted the latest sighting on Facebook – a 3-plus minute video shot above the Home Depot area of the plaza at just after 7 p.m." Author's note – the video is no longer available on Pittaro's *Facebook* page. The article continued, "Pittaro stated in the recording that he was unable to see the orbs with the naked eye but when looking through his camera, could see the orbs clearly. The video was shot after the sun was setting and dusk began to set in. Pittaro noted that he and his wife had irregularly taken photos of the sunset but had never seen anything like this before. 'My wife started taking photos of the sunset and caught the UFOs,' he wrote in the thread. 'These objects were NOT visible to the naked eye. After asking multiple people to use their cellphones, they too caught the exact same UFOs, verifying what we were recording. My wife and I have a good amount of video and photos between us, and what I shared here is what I felt was the best of what we filmed.'" Author's note – While the video cannot be located on *Facebook*, the video and still images can be viewed on Pittaro's Flickr account. Go to *Flickr.com* and search, "UFOs Concord, NH". Schinella continued, "At one point in the video, some lights broke off from the main cluster and then a couple of minutes later, reappeared. Pittaro had a friend enlarge some screenshots from the original video in order to examine the orbs up close. The enlargements revealed silver-gray metal masses with rounded edges. More than 3,000 people have shared the video on Facebook since it was posted. Other commenters in the thread also stated that they had seen the light orbs previously in the sky, too."

March 11, 2016 – The Mall of New Hampshire, located in Manchester, was the site of another sighting caught on camera. *Patch.com* once again reported the encounter. "The most recent sighting was over the Queen City, 'a saucer-like object,' that was pulsating and slowly moving over the western part of the city toward Bedford…." The footage was captured in a parking lot toward South Willow Street and was witnessed by multiple people at the mall that evening. Five days before this sighting, another was reported. "On March 6, 2016, another light in the sky with a halo shape around it was reported from the Concord Heights area, near where other pulsating objects were seen in September 2015, outside of the Steeplegate Mall. The trackers followed the object from Concord along Route 28 east but reported losing track of it." The light was reportedly seen later that night in Pittsfield, New Hampshire. A month prior to this sighting, another witness reported a strange sighting in Milford. The article continued, "In Milford in late February, a commenter noted that there were two purple lights in the sky that he assumed to be planes until one doubled back on itself and began changing altitude. He thought they might be drones but were flying pretty high and cutting at various angles in the sky. 'They would come close to each other (then separate),' he noted." That same month, another sighting was reported out of Salem, New Hampshire, "…another witness reported seeing a 'bright ball of light' in the sky along with other small aircraft that appeared to be on normal flight paths. The ball of light, however, 'flew quickly over our heads' and then a second object appeared and faded off into the distance. Others have also reported seeing lights in the skies above Salem and Methuen, MA, in mid-February and posted videos on YouTube. In Bow, residents reported in early January that they were walking their dog when they saw a pink flash and then a red light that passed directly over their heads, at a low altitude. They then saw multiple lights but there was no noise. The four lights appeared to be traveling in different directions across 20 miles toward Concord, according to the online report."

In establishing the construct of the historic reports of Betty and Barney Hill, the children from the gravel pit, the children from the sledding hill, and the incident at Exeter, then layering in these recent reports, in my opinion, circles us back to "inconceivable" reconstructing to "conceivable". Especially when looking at the Mike Stevens case from 1983, we're barely a decade removed from those earlier encounters when Mike's first encounter happened. The thought process here is to not win over a skeptic or to convince anyone of any of these encounters, including Mike's. Instead, it's about kindness, respect, a non-judgmental ear, and a rational open mind that can guide us when interacting with a person who is surviving trauma. I'm a survivor, so is Mike, and so are many others. We faulter, sometimes often. We need support, sometimes often. We also want to be happy. If we're here, we're choosing life. If we're here, we have a story. Mike and few others are willing to share those stories, so let's just listen.

Intruders
(1987-1990)

The Simpsons burst onto the scene in 1989 with staggering ratings for the relatively new broadcast network, Fox Television. The show parodies everything from American culture to the human condition itself. An episode from 1997 titled, *The Springfield Files*, featured *X-Files* characters Dana Scully and Fox Mulder as they attempted to investigate an alien encounter that Homer reported. Hilarity ensued as no one believed Homer and he's ridiculed throughout the episode. He stayed steadfast in his account because he knew what he experienced was real. It's eventually revealed that the alien is nothing more than Mr. Burns who had received "longevity treatments", which caused his odd appearance.

Diehard fans will know that *The Simpsons*' debut was actually in 1987 when it appeared as an animated short for the television program, *The Tracey Ullman Show*. That same year, extreme weather events pounded the Earth. The Great Storm of 1987 was a tropical cyclone that had hurricane-force winds and killed numerous people across England, France and the Channel Islands. Hurricane Emily was the catalyst for The Great Storm and was the singular hurricane of significance that developed during a reported below-average 1987 hurricane season. It originally formed out of a tropical disturbance that moved off the west coast of Africa. Over in the United States, heavy rains plagued much of Maine, Massachusetts and New Hampshire. According to the *United States Geological Survey* website, "The flooding was the result of two distinct storms – one that brought heavy rains to the area from March 30 to April 2 and the other that brought additional precipitation from April 4 through April 8." Precipitation wasn't the only thing descending from the skies that year; Mike Stevens was visited for a second time.

Around the time of the weather disturbances overseas, Mike was at his home in South Hampton, New Hampshire. His house was located next door to his grandmother's (the site of his 1983 encounter) and his bedroom window faced her home. While lying in bed one night, Mike spied a ball of light outside his window. He looked on as the pane of glass softly illuminated and Mike became confused as to what it might be. Suddenly, the ball multiplied and entered his bedroom through the window. He stated in our interview, "Once they got into the room, they would form into these smoky silhouettes of bodies. You couldn't really see any features to them; it almost looked like a living shadow made out of smoke or something." He watched as these entities formed in his room and was able to discern that four of them were present. He said that their bodies were humanoid shadows with wispy smoke-like movement inside of them, but they were not always perceived as humanoid. He continued, "I'm not sure of the right words. They had 'characters' or 'tells' that gave you the impression of what they were. You could see them without seeing them. I got the impression that two of them were male, one was a female and one was a small male child." Mike said that these entities visited him quite often, happening at least three times per week and lasted over the course of nine months. A routine developed, and it all became normal for him. Mike said of the beginning visits, "Typically, what would happen is the two males would stand by the edge of my bed, the long side. The female would pace in the corner and then the boy would sit on the floor near the head of my bed." They communicated with him telepathically and Mike explained that their visits were educational in nature and included different types of lessons. He feels as though a mental block or something similar was placed onto his memory preventing him from recollecting what the lessons were about. "The two males seemed militaristic," Mike added, "not in an aggressive or warring way but in a strict, he-needs-to-learn-his-lessons type thing, he needs to know this, he needs to understand it. Although that was the impression, I don't have any clue what the lessons were. I'm just left with my impression of the situation and I can't remember any details."

As the weeks and months went on, Mike recalled one of their visits where he was allowed to interact with the child entity. He said of the interaction, "I was allowed to get off of the bed and sit with the boy. I remember asking or thinking, 'What are you?' Then all of a sudden, I just got this image of Rosy the Robot from *The Jetsons*… like, beamed into my head. I don't think we physically laughed but there was like an overwhelming expression of joy, almost like we laughed internally without physically laughing. I didn't know what to make of it. I think at the time I thought it was a joke." There was another visitation where Mike remembered that the female entity showed him something peculiar. He said, "The female approached the bed and she showed me a little box, a little smaller than a shoe box. She opened it up, and when she opened it, inside it looked almost like an arrowhead, but it looked like it was made out of crystal or glass or something, and she told me, 'This is the key.' And I never knew what that meant, if it was a physical key or a metaphorical symbolism to something." In my research, I found that the arrowhead is said to symbolize a few different ideas. One is alertness, and according to the *Legend of America* website, "Arrowheads may be made of numerous types of stones and the sizes and styles varied widely depending upon the intended use. Regardless of which stone arrowheads are carved from, Native Americans have long believed that wearing a hand-carved arrowhead, as a talisman around the neck, is a symbol of protection, courage and strength." I like to think that's why the entity showed it to him or, perhaps, kept it for him.

Mike explained that as time went on, and especially toward the end of the visitations, only one male entity would appear. However, on the last night they visited him, everything was in contrast to prior visits. All entities were there, and the visitation did not start in his room. Mike stated, "The last time I saw them, the scenario was different because it didn't start in the bedroom." Mike had no idea where he was when he awoke this time. He was confused and tried to look around, but his vision was obstructed. Mike said, "All I could see was this white cloth and I saw blood on it. I figured out the blood was coming from my nose." He wiped his nose and looked around, it was at that point he realized that he was in the air, floating outside of his home. He continued, "I could look around and see the back stairs that went to the mud room, which you had to cut through to get to my bedroom. I pulled back, I realized that white cloth was some type of garment/robe that this female entity was wearing. I don't remember getting from there, in the air, into the house. The next thing I remember, I'm in the house, I'm in my room." As far as the lesson plan for that night, there was none, and he felt that the two males were alarmed. "For once, there didn't seem to be a plan. You could sense panic in them. Along with that, I could actually physically see them this time." Mike was surprised by this and studied their features as much as he could. He had never seen them so clearly before. He said of their appearance, "The males, I would guess to be about five feet, kinda your typical grey alien look with the bigger head, bigger eyes. But they were more… skin was like white, purple-blue hue to it…" He could see that the skin of the males seemed flawed but that the female entity's skin was not. He added, "She looked pretty much like them except she was a little shorter and her features were more polished. They were more smooth…" "…there weren't as many physical flaws in her skin." In my opinion, I think it would be fair to connect their blue hue skin color to the "blue infant skin". It's a conjecture or supposition at best, but interesting to think about.

Mike overwhelmingly felt their tensioned and panicked state which only added to his confusion. He got the impression that there may have been an abduction attempt by another extraterrestrial sect or species and that his regular visitors interrupted that abduction, which, he thought, might not be allowed. In what sense? Mike was unsure. He felt unsure about the entire event. He told me, "They are all just pacing around, frantic. I don't remember them leaving. But that was the last time those visits happened. I don't know for sure; my impression of the situation is that they interceded or got in the middle of something they weren't supposed to…."

I pushed it a little more and asked, "So would you say they may have intervened with another species or something else that was trying to abduct you?" Mike said, "Another species, another sect, I don't know. But that's the impression that I got, yeah."

During the time of those visitations, Mike also had a nightmarish recurring dream about a wall of glowing, white arms trying to grab him. He's not aware of any correlation to the entities and it could have simply been a way for his brain to process everything that was happening to him. In the same breath, we could also infer a potential abstract connection with abduction and the arms are representative of alien intruders. Mike said, "I was having recurring nightmares. I used to call them gorilla arms. It just would be like a wall of arms, not like two or three, ya know, the whole wall. Just these white glowing arms trying to grab me. I don't think any of them ever touched me but just the dream locked me in fear..."

Frighteners in Farmington

About a year after those visitations ended, Mike and his family moved to Farmington, New Hampshire. We had driven there too, that day of our second interview. He lived in multiple homes there and the town was our last stop on the little tour of Mike's encounter locations that we were taking. Our first stop in Farmington was to be at the home he lived in when he was around 10 or 11 years old. Mike sat in the passenger seat as I drove. I flipped on the radio; it must have been a pop station because Billie Eilish's *Ocean Eyes* was playing. I wasn't mad at that. I got love for Billie, and our bellies were full after our lunch at the Far Out Diner located in Dover, New Hampshire, so we were quite content. As the sky stormed and dropped fresh snow onto the road, we drove in relative silence. Mike lit a cigarette; I had quit about two years prior and the smell was intoxicating. I considered asking for one but shook off the thought. I sipped my coffee and looked for a gas station. I don't know the area well, so I'm not sure where we stopped, but it was at that time I got an overwhelming feeling of empathy for Mike. He was sharing intimate and highly unusual encounters with me. I was thankful for his trust and impressed at his bravery.

Back on the road and in Farmington, we pulled up to the house of his next encounter. It was quaint and unassuming, and there was a little plastic snowman decoration out front. I thought it to be gaudy; I did not ask Mike for his thoughts. While there, again, Mike shared a brief overview of the encounter, and I snapped a few pictures. During the interview I asked, "This was around '89-'90 would you say?" "Yeah," he responded, "it happened a little while after we had moved in. I looked out the back window to the backyard. It was the middle of the night; I don't know why I got up to do this. I looked out the window and I saw five little troll-looking things. And by troll, I guess they were like 3 feet tall, and just kinda wrinkled up with a pug face. They still had the big black eyes like the common greys do but it wasn't as pronounced. They were wearing what looked like garden gnome style clothes. Like made out of a burlap sack, a very rustic look, I guess? Each of them had a spade shovel in their hand that was proportionally sized to them. They're all standing around with their shovels, and in front of each one of them was a hole. The hole was smaller than the shovel and it looked like a perfectly cored circle." Mike was troubled at the site before him. Despite this, he managed to study as much detail as possible. Besides the creatures themselves, Mike studied how odd the holes seemed. They were just too perfect, and their shovels were entirely too large to have made them. As he watched the creatures, an odd feeling occurred to him. He continued, "My impression was that it was some type of…. It was like a screen memory except I knew it was false as I was watching it happen. To me it almost seemed like, whatever was there, was playing cleanup. Like they were the cleanup crew to make sure they didn't leave tracks or evidence, that sort of thing." Mike recalls nothing further from that night. In fact, he has no memory of them leaving or of going back to bed. He said, "I remember waking up and life was normal the next day."

A couple months after the "troll" encounter, another peculiar event occurred. It was early in the evening; Mike was in his bedroom standing near his window melting crayons. It wasn't so much a hobby but rather something he did to pass the time. While he was doing this, a face appeared in the bedroom window. He shared with me, "I was standing there doing that one night, it was, I'd say it was probably early evening, barely dark. All of a sudden, this giant face appeared in the window. The face took up the whole window. It's on the second floor, I think it was more of a projection of some type than an actual, physical creature. I remember it just staring at me, I don't think it lasted very long, 30-45 seconds maybe. As I'm staring at it, it's staring at me, and this blue jay comes crashing through this face and into the window like inches from my face. When this happens, the face disappears, and I just completely freaked out."

When I got back to my hotel room after

interviewing Mike, I did some research on blue jay symbolism. The *Dreaming and Sleeping* website stated, "Blue jay is a symbol of communication, intelligence and curiosity. It means that blue jay people are very intelligent and determined. This bird may also symbolize protection and fearlessness. If a blue jay appears in your life, you will feel safe and protected." In my opinion, that seems similar to the arrowhead symbolism. And perhaps this symbolism came crashing into his life as a reminder to not be scared, to know that all that is happening to him is for a reason. Again, it is impossible to know any of this; I'm a third-party bystander and I'm just processing it myself, from my own perspective. It's difficult, confusing, fascinating, and ornate. I'm actually not quite sure what to do with all of the information that Mike has provided to me, other than to follow his wishes and share it with all of you. But it's more than just sharing. It's like experiencing a portion of his encounters. It is just so utterly intimate, just the fact that he's sharing makes us all a part of his inner circle.

    A few days removed from the frightening image in the window, Mike realized the face looked familiar to him. He told me, "I had seen that face somewhere before. My grandfather was huge about us reading. He lived in New Jersey, we went down at least once a year and every time we did there'd be a trip to the bookstore. I picked out this book a couple of years back that had an alien on the cover. I never read it at the time, it was above my reading level. It was the book *Intruders* by Budd Hopkins." Mike said the face on Hopkins' original 1987 cover shared a striking similarity to the face that appeared in his window. If you're not familiar with the book, I would recommend you conduct a *Google Image* search for it. If you've done that, just imagine the terror that it would inflict. Then just as you're trying to comprehend that image in front of you, a loud and violent action occurs. I don't care who you are, that's terrifying, that's upsetting, and it was upsetting to Mike. In his own words, he "freaked out." Regardless of our opinion on whether or not this actually occurred, his perception is what matters. His well-being and mental health are what's at stake. In my opinion, that's a big deal, especially when considering the person, not the proof, as Mike does. This book is not a scientific study of the UFO phenomena, it's telling the story of one man's encounters. You decide what you want to believe.

Dreamcatcher
(1991-1992)

A little over a year went by without incident, at least none that he could remember. Mike and his family had moved to Middleton, New Hampshire and all had settled in. Extraterrestrial activity was never far removed from Mike's mind, and although he thought about it from time to time, he could never predict how it might present itself.

In this new house, Mike's bedroom window faced the woods. He was and still is a lover of all things nature and often looked out his window when trying to fall asleep. One night, while lying in bed, he noticed an out-of-place light in amongst the trees. He saw it on numerous occasions and described it to me as, "Where my bed was facing the backwoods, I would see a light out there dancing around in the woods. It was a tiny light, not big enough to be able to go, 'oh it's this or it's that or whatever'. My dad would say it was just somebody on their ATV." Mike decided to go out during the day to see if he could figure out what the cause for the light might be. He continued, "I had gone out into the woods during the daylight and there weren't trails out there; there wasn't room for that." Mike explained this to his father who, in turn, provided Mike with a scope from an old rifle so his boy could try and get a better look. Mike tried numerous times to get the light in the scope's field of vision, but he struggled. This worried Mike because, beyond his curiosity, he wanted to keep an eye on it. He shared, "I was trying to figure out what it was and keep an eye on it so it couldn't keep an eye on me. I'm not really sure what my plan was… it was kinda like a self-preservation thing. I had to know what it was doing there." The story is innocuous enough, but Mike's feeling of "self-preservation" put things into perspective. Lights were more than just lights for him. After his previous encounters, I couldn't blame him. This story of his also reminded me of someone else who saw a light in the woods. Its outcome is one of the scariest and strangest stories I have ever heard. It happened in my home state and I'll share a brief retelling of it here.

In the book, *Real Wolfmen: True Encounters in Modern America,* author and researcher Linda Godfrey related a story of a terrifying night in Palmyra, Maine. In the late summer of 2007, Eric and Shelly Martin moved into a new home and were unpacking one evening. Eric walked by a window and a light out in the woods caught his eye. He peered out into the woods, trying to understand what he was seeing. He observed a ball of light floating throughout the trees. He couldn't figure out what it was and called his wife over to get her thoughts. When she looked, the light was gone. Eric explained to her what he saw, and they figured that it could be people or, worse, poachers with flashlights. The next day, Eric had his son go out to the woods to see if he could find any evidence of what could have been out there; he came back emptyhanded. As time went on, the lights became a common occurrence until one night, something else was observed outside their window. When Eric heard some unusual sounds coming from his backyard, he flicked on the outside light and went to the window to see what it was. His eyes widened when he saw five pairs of glowing eyes staring back at him just beyond his porch and just out of reach of the light. At first, he thought they might be a pack of dogs or maybe wolves, given how large they appeared to him. Shelly looked on from the living room, unsure at what Eric was seeing. He looked back at her, his face furrowed with worry. She walked toward him, looking out the window. They looked on in horror as five werewolf-like beings began to stand bipedally, snarling and staring. In their estimation, some of the creatures were seven feet tall. Their daughter slept upstairs, unaware of the happenings outside so Eric and Shelly ran to her, making sure that she was safe. They described the wolves as skulking about the property for most of the night. They came onto the porch and thought they could hear at least one on the roof. At one point, they looked outside from an upstairs window and observed a sixth, smaller creature on the back of one of the larger ones. They felt helpless in defending themselves and stayed up all night. Just before day broke, the creatures left.

The werewolf-like description in their story is known within the fringes of cryptozoology as "Dogmen". Thousands of encounters have been reported and describe similar events, some even more terrifying. Godfrey has even written about a potential extraterrestrial connection to the Dogmen phenomena. An article from the *Mysterious Universe* website reported, "In 2005, Linda was contacted by a man – a military whistle-blower, we might say – who was an expert in the field of remote-viewing. Essentially, remote-viewing is a process that allows the mind to psychically travel to just about here, there and everywhere. Astral travel, one might say. According to Godfrey's Edward Snowden-like source, the U.S. Government has uncovered data suggesting that the Dogmen are a very ancient, alien race that closely resembles the ancient deity of the Underworld, Anubis. Godfrey's informant also discovered – via remote-viewing – that the Dogmen can 'jump' from location to location via portals or doorways in the fabric of space and time." I wonder if lights in the woods could be a sign of those portals, or the Dogmen themselves? Perhaps Mike's feeling of "self-preservation" is connected to that. Or, it was just a flashlight from someone walking in the woods.

After some time, Mike didn't see the light anymore. Instead of being able to relish in that fact, he began having more dreams. Peculiar dreams with an extraterrestrial theme. He told me about a recurring one he described as, "In this dream, I was out in my parents' driveway out in the road, the main road, the front of the house. From up and down the woods all the way down this dirt road there were like these giant crafts or UFOs. They were almost staged, like one was high one was low, staggered like how horses are on a carousel but not in a circle, in a straight line all the way up and down the woods and road. Nothing happened, they didn't move or anything. But it was a weird dream-like situation."

Runnin' Down a Dream

If that wasn't enough, Mike had another dream, this one stranger than the last. He told me, "I don't know how or why, but I was on this train. The inside of the train was shiny, like a lot of chrome, almost looked like a mix between a '50s styled diner and a train. Passengers, they all looked like they were wearing '50s styled clothing, like the hats and overcoats. But on their coats and skin there was this purple-silver dust and the skin look mummified. So, I'd go from car to car, I don't know how many I walked through, it was quite a few. Finally, I got to a car that was different and it had… almost like a bunch of medics from World War I or something. It was an older style military operation and they were moving around in a panic or more like a purpose. Then I went to another car, it was still the train, but it opened up to this room, too. This room or train car, whatever you want to call it, was just lined with medical/surgical operating tables. On the tables, there were bodies of aliens. You could clearly see just by looking at them that they were all dead. I think there were two cars like that and that was really the end of it. I don't know what to make of it."

The website *Psychology Today* published an article about a Freudian relationship between dreams and people's belief in aliens. The article prefaced with, "When asked about dreams where one views the death of a loved one, Freud posited that they might be disguised wish-fulfillment. For example, unconscious hostility towards that loved one might have been repressed into the unconscious because it was probably an unacceptable thought to the conscious ego. Because Freud had a kind of hydraulic view of emotions, repressed thoughts would arise in dreams when there was little conscious control…." When you relate this to a belief in aliens, the suggestion is that dreams are simply an unconscious fulfilment of that conscious thought. A study was done, "years ago" according to the article, which compared and contrasted groups of people who believe in aliens and people who do not. The article said of the study, "…it was found that, on the whole, those who believed they had been abducted by aliens were no crazier, stranger, or neurotic than people who did not believe they had been abducted by aliens. Apparently, the only characteristic that distinguished between the two groups was a belief in aliens…." The point of the article being, there is a possibility for people who believe in aliens might just be experiencing "Freudian wish fulfilling dreams". Of course, this is possible, but the article further clarified that, "There are at least three reasons that may aid in the plausibility of this hypothesis; (1) the reports of alien abductions are often during the night when a person could be dreaming. Of course, people may take naps at any point in the day, so they could dream about aliens at any time but predominantly aliens appear to have a preference for abductions when it's dark and when people are sleeping in the dark; (2) because some of the more logical and critical-thinking parts of our brains (i.e., dorsolateral prefrontal cortex) are inactive during dream sleep, we rarely challenge the notion that when we are dreaming, they are simply dreams and not real. We are frightened by scary things, we are sad by unhappy things, and we are joyful when happy things occur in our dreams. Thus, in a wish-fulfilling dream of aliens, it would be highly unusual if we challenged the reality of finally meeting aliens in our dreams; and (3) it is interesting that so many alien-abduction reports contain stories of being paralyzed by the aliens. The paralysis is consistent with the well-established finding that REM sleep is accompanied by muscle atonia (i.e., muscle paralysis), which appears to be an evolutionarily evolved device to keep humans from acting out their dreams during REM sleep."

A contrasting view of this comes from a 1990 Harvard study. It was performed by the head of the department of psychiatry at Harvard Medical School, John E. Mack. He conducted a psychological study of people who experienced alien abductions. According to a journal article from the *National Center for Biotechnology Information, U.S. National Library of Medicine*, Mack interviewed 200 men and women for the study. The article spoke to his interest and outcome of the study, it stated, "His interest in the stories of people who said they had been abducted by aliens—he called them his 'experiencers'—began in

1990. He told an interviewer, 'When I heard about this phenomenon in 1990, I was very doubtful. I thought it must be some kind of mental illness.' He later described the abduction claims as 'an authentic mystery that deserved to be researched.'" Alien abduction is not often an area of study from academic figures, especially with the esteem that Mack was held in at Harvard Medical School. The journal article continued, "Elizabeth Loftus, professor of psychology at the University of California, Irvine, and an expert in the malleability of memory, said that Dr Mack 'underestimated his own role in creating the recollections and beliefs' of his patients. 'His use of hypnosis gave the method undeserved credibility.' Dr Mack shrugged off demands for physical evidence, saying such demands were merely part of a flawed 'Western' construct of science that failed to appreciate 'other dimensions'—dimensions that he said could not be measured or proved by ordinary means. By listening to patients carefully, Dr Mack claimed he could determine that their stories were true and not explainable by other phenomena such as mental illness, sleep paralysis, seizures, or dreams."

Because of those beliefs and purported radical methods he used, Harvard Medical School launched an investigation into his alien abduction study. The journal article stated, "Dr Mack, who founded the department of psychiatry at Cambridge Hospital, Massachusetts, in the late 1960s and became professor of psychiatry at Harvard in 1972, faced potential loss of tenure because of his unconventional methods. Harvard authorities launched an inquiry into his work in 1994. The review committee was headed by Arnold Relman, former editor of the New England Journal of Medicine and professor of medicine at Harvard. He told the BMJ, 'We quickly came to the conclusion that he had the right to investigate any issue he wanted, no matter how weird. After all, Galileo sounded weird to many people of his day. But we did believe he should use rational and scholarly methods.' In an interview with the BBC, Mack was asked about his personal belief in alien abduction, he said 'I would never say, yes, there are aliens taking people. [But] I would say there is a compelling powerful phenomenon here that I can't account for in any other way, that's mysterious. Yet I can't know what it is but it seems to me that it invites a deeper, further inquiry.'"

In my opinion, Mike's actions within Granite Sky Services echo those of Mack's study; people not proof. While controversial to some, there is a fairness contained in that; people are heard. That's a powerful win for survivors of trauma.

Granite Skies Picture Section

The former home of Mike's grandmother. South Hampton, NH.

The UFO in Mike's first encounter hovered over this telephone pole. South Hampton, NH.

The lot of Mike's childhood home; site of numerous visitations in 1987. South Hampton, NH.

Home where Mike witnessed trolls with shovels and the face in the window in 1989-1990. Farmington, NH.

Upper right window that Mike looked out and saw the trolls and where the alien face appeared in 1989-1990. Farmington, NH.

The home where Mike saw the creature in his living room in 2001. Farmington, NH.

This is the home that Mike sleepwalked to in 2005. Farmington, NH.

The tree that the creature in the driveway peered from in 2005-2006. Farmington, NH.

Former KRI Center, Stratham, NH.

Mike Stevens, 2020.

A young Mike Stevens with his grandfather.

Trail cam pic of the cabin where the beam of light was captured. Control pic.

Beam of light captured on the trail cam.

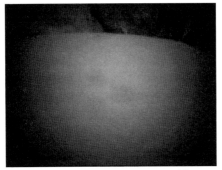

Three marks on Mike's ex-wife.

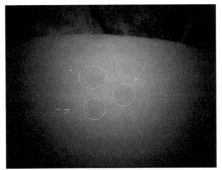

Same picture outlining where the markings are for clarity.

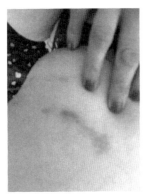
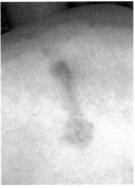

Bruising on Mike's ex-girlfriend's thigh.

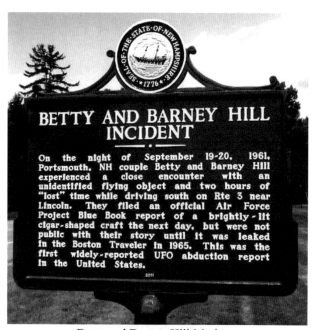

Betty and Barney Hill Marker.

Mike, Valerie, and Shannon at the cabin where they saw the UFO.

Piece of plane wreckage hung in Mike's office. Artwork on wreckage by artist Roger Tirrell.

Mike with plane wreckage out in the woods.

Mike & Nomar.

Sign in Mike's office.

Banner in Mike's office.

More signage in Mike's office.

Nomar Slevik outside of the Far Out Diner, 2019.

THE OLD MAN OF THE MOUNTAIN.

The Chronicles of Nonsense
(1994-1998)

*T*he coastal Maine community of Belfast once had a string of UFO sightings starting in 1968. A teenager named Tom and his friends witnessed odd, aerial crafts during the fall and winter. Tom said of their first sighting, "…we noticed a lighted object coming along approximately one hundred feet above the power line. The object came from the east and when a few hundred yards away from us, it halted still above the power lines. We heard no sound… we saw the object spin about. It was of a basic, elliptical shape. It was lit with red and green lights and appeared to have windows." While the object hovered, it started to release smaller, bright objects from beneath it. Days later, when they returned to the area, the object did as well. Tom said, "This became a regular habit, and we went almost every night. About half the time, we were rewarded by seeing similar objects acting in much the same way as during our initial sighting. In fact, seeing these things became routine and we became desensitized to it. In time, we began to bring others with us to see the objects. On some nights, we would see multiple objects. Each one followed the power lines. Never, did one deviate from this pattern."

On one particular evening, Tom and a friend took their dates to the area to see if the UFO would appear. They parked and drank a little and then the UFO arrived. Tom explained, "We decided to leave the car and walk down toward the object. Before leaving, we made sure to put our beer on the floor in back and I took off my coat and covered it, so anyone walking up to the car would not see it. We walked down toward the object and the girls became frightened and refused to go any further. So, we stood there, watching this large object hover over the power lines. It was huge and the girls were speechless. This was the closest any of us had ever been to one of these. I was able to make out movement inside the craft, although again, the forms were vague and indistinct." The next morning Tom remembered his jacket and went to the car to get it. He searched around but couldn't find it anywhere in the car. It wasn't until he got down on his hands and knees and looked under the seat that he saw the jacket and tugged on the sleeve. Oddly, that was the only portion found in the car. Tom said of the coat, "This was a sheepskin-lined, corduroy coat, something like 'The Marlboro Man' wore. And someone had pulled the arm off it… think it was the left arm. Little threads stuck out at different angles, which made me think that whoever did this was very strong." Tom drove back to the "UFO area" and when he approached where they usually parked, he saw what he thought to be a dead animal in the road. He drove around it and parked his car. When he got out, he looked at the thing in the road and realized it wasn't an animal at all. While he walked cautiously closer, a realization came over him, it was the rest of his coat. Tom described the area that morning as having a fresh dusting of snow, though none on the jacket. He said that there were no tire tracks or footprints in the area at all, other than the ones he created that morning. He was bewildered at how his coat was there and left the area frightened. He said, "I was practically paralyzed with fear. I backed around and left as fast as I could. I have not been back to that place since, although I live only a few miles away." Tom and his friends never reported any missing time or thought they had been abducted, but the incident with the jacket haunted him. It implied to him that something more may have happened and has considered hypnotic regression.

Wallet & Pants

Like Tom, Mike had an incident with missing clothes. He was fifteen years old at the time and living in Middleton, New Hampshire. He woke up one morning and couldn't find his wallet and the pants he had worn to a friend's house the previous day. He searched his room and figured he must have dropped the wallet while walking back from his friend's house. During that time, Mike shared that he and his buddies walked the neighbourhood often and knew the landscape well. He said, "We all knew the trails. I walked home, which was typical, it wasn't far, maybe a mile." Mike was much more concerned about the wallet than the pants and headed out to find it. He told me, "I decided I'd backtrack. I must have dropped it, I know which way I came, ya know? So, I'm like alright, I better just get up and go out there and find it before someone else does." While walking, he got this odd feeling that his wallet *and* pants were up a little side road where a house was being built at the time. The sensation washed over him as an absolute fact. He said of the incident, "Just over halfway to this place, there's a side road and up that side road, they were building a new house. They just poured the foundation, but they hadn't quite started building the house. As I got up to that road, I just had this weird idea that's where they were. It suddenly made complete sense, that's where they would be even though I didn't go anywhere near it. So, I went to the foundation, I walked around and looked and didn't find anything. I was flabbergasted, and I was out of ideas and didn't understand why they weren't there." Mike, like Tom, had a sense that something more happened than what was remembered. But unlike Tom, Mike never found his wallet or pants.

A few years later, around the same age Tom had been during his encounters, Mike and a couple of friends had a strange night while on their way to visit a buddy in college.

The Beer Bottle

In the fall of 1997, Mike and some buddies were headed down to the University of New Hampshire to visit a friend who had just started their freshman year. They were enjoying one another and blasting music as they laughed and drove. Mike said, "We were going down on a Friday night, me and two other buddies." As Mike drove, a weird shape in the sky caught his attention. He continued to share with me, "I was driving, one was in the front, one was in the back. On our way, there was this pond, kind of a swampy area and there's a little overpass, not quite a bridge." As I listened and typed away on my laptop, I'm transported into Mike's car. I again find myself in the moment, and I am now watching the scene unfold before me. Mike continued, "There's a guard rail and a streetlamp there and as we're driving past it, and this is on the passenger side of the car, I noticed this little glimpse of something. So, I pulled over." I metaphorically crane my neck to see the streetlamp. I see a small, dark body of water… I can only imagine what Mike saw next. He told me, "We all get out of the car. We're all standing on the curb, against the guardrail, looking out over the swamp. None of us are seeing anything, one of us says, 'What are we doing? Let's just get going.' As we started to move to go back to the car, we turned just enough that the streetlight wasn't blinding our view so much and we caught this curved shape, like half a ball. It was a silvery reflection or something. I pointed and said, 'There it is!'"

In my imagination, I look skyward with Mike and his friends. Having not been there, I pictured a half moon and interrupted the conversation by asking him if it was possible that it was the moon. He shot me a look and said, "It definitely wasn't, we all clearly saw it from the car at one point and this looked nothing like it." I researched the moon phases for September of 1997 and during the time of their road trip, the moon was just exiting a "waxing gibbus" on its way to a full moon. This would have put the moon's area of visibility at approximately 76-85% visible; obviously more than a "first quarter" or half-moon. I then asked him, "What happened next?"

He was fidgeting with a small, 8-ounce bottle of water and said, "The next thing I know, we're all back in the car. I'm in the front seat. Both of my friends are in the back seat. They've just got these frozen faces of fear on them. This image of a grey, typical alien kind of appears in front of me and then I got the image of this broken beer bottle." I stopped typing at this point and looked up at him. I'm sure my face was contorted with a confused look. He said, "The next thing I know, the three of us are outside the car again in between the car and the guardrail." I picture the scene and continue with my notes. He said, "I look down by the tire closest to the curb and there is a broken beer bottle. So, we decide that's what I saw, that's why I must have pulled over. We get in the car and drive on and continue the night, like nothing ever happened because that seemed like a reasonable excuse at the time." I finished my notes on the encounter and asked him, "Do you think the imagery of the broken beer bottle was a screen memory?" He didn't hesitate and said, "Yeah, I think so. I don't even know if the beer bottle was there at all, and they just went along with it as an excuse because that would be a lot easier to handle, ya know?"

In my notes I wrote, "what a weird thing to use for a screen memory."

Mike added, "Looking back, I saw something in the sky. Not once, but twice, once driving and once standing there. There's no way I pulled over because of a broken beer bottle on the side of the road. It just doesn't make any sense at all, but at the time, just to rationalize it enough to move on, I think that's what we all did."

The Praying Mantis

The following year, Mike experienced an event that triggered his trauma. Of note, before moving on, I wanted to briefly discuss the meaning of the word "triggered" in regard to trauma. Often times, the word is used flippantly. I have found that what a person typically means when they use that word is that something merely upset them for a brief moment. An example of an erroneous use of "triggered" would be, "That song is so annoying, I'm triggered!" While certain song lyrics may have insensitive material that could cause a reminder of an awful situation that an individual survived and could "trigger" symptoms of their anxiety or post-traumatic stress disorder, it's been my experience, when someone uses the word in that manner, it's another way to say that they are mad, upset, or otherwise perturbed by a certain person, action, thing, etc. In regard to mental health, forms of the word "trigger" relate to PTSD, anxiety, panic, and more. The *Good Therapy* website stated, "A trigger in psychology is a stimulus such as a smell, sound, or sight that triggers feelings of trauma. People typically use this term when describing post-traumatic stress (PTSD)." And, "A trigger is a reminder of a past trauma. This reminder can cause a person to feel overwhelming sadness, anxiety, or panic. It may also cause someone to have flashbacks. A flashback is a vivid, often negative memory that may appear without warning. It can cause someone to lose track of their surroundings and 'relive" a traumatic event."

Mike's event occurred in Rochester, New Hampshire in 1998. He was washing dishes one evening when something quite ordinary scared him. He shared, "I was living in Rochester at the time, second floor apartment. We weren't supposed to smoke in the apartment, but I was doing the dumb bachelor thing where you use every dish in the house, so the time had come to get them all washed. So, I just opened up the window and leaned out to have a cigarette. When I did this, there was a praying mantis on the side of the window. It startled me, and caught me off-guard, which you might expect in that situation."

A personal admission to all of you is that I am terrified of insects and knew exactly what he meant. Also, I'll admit, that I probably would have screamed. But the following action from Mike surprised even himself. He said, "What I didn't expect is that at the same time, I grabbed a knife off the cabinet that was right there and sliced it in half. It was an instant reaction, it wasn't thought out, it just happened. The fact that I did that freaked me out more than the bug scaring me itself." I asked him if he could further explain what that meant, he said, "I'm usually pretty good about animals and insects. They don't normally freak me out. This reaction was deeper, like a subconscious triggering event or something." I asked him if that meant that it could relate to his extraterrestrial trauma. He said that he feels that it does, and that the praying mantis reminded him of his past alien intruders in some way. Either by the look of the insect itself, or the manner in which it scared him, he's not entirely sure.

Silver Linings
(2000-2006)

The Y2K bug or the "millennium bug" was a perceived computer issue that many users thought would cause technical malfunctions in their systems with dates beyond December 31, 1999. The *National Geographic* reported, "When complicated computer programs were being written during the 1960s through the 1980s, computer engineers used a two-digit code for the year. The "19" was left out. Instead of a date reading 1970, it read 70. Engineers shortened the date because data storage in computers was costly and took up a lot of space. As the year 2000 approached, computer programmers realized that computers might not interpret 00 as 2000, but as 1900. Activities that were programmed on a daily or yearly basis would be damaged or flawed. As December 31, 1999, turned into January 1, 2000, computers might interpret December 31, 1999, turning into January 1, 1900." It seemed like the whole world was abuzz at the impending doom the computer malfunction would cause the world. I actually remember having a conversation with my father on New Year's Eve in 1999, pondering this same concern. He said something like, "I'm sure it'll be no big deal."

As it turned out, he was right. The Y2K bug was mostly a nonissue. *National Geographic* wrote, "In the end, there were very few problems. A nuclear energy facility in Ishikawa, Japan, had some of its radiation equipment fail, but backup facilities ensured there was no threat to the public. The U.S. detected missile launches in Russia and attributed that to the Y2K bug. But the missile launches were planned ahead of time as part of Russia's conflict in its republic of Chechnya. There was no computer malfunction. Countries such as Italy, Russia, and South Korea had done little to prepare for Y2K. They had no more technological problems than those countries, like the U.S., that spent millions of dollars to combat the problem."

Fatherhood

Another significant event of the millennium, at least in Mike Stevens' world, was the birth of his daughter on December 2, 2000. Fatherhood, though it didn't come easy, was a welcomed change for Mike. He said of that time in his life, "It was a mix of excitement and terror. I was a 21-year-old kid. I wasn't sure I was ready for this…" He had experience in co-parenting his then fiancée's four-year-old son but felt the birth of his own flesh and blood was life changing. He continued, "It was mind blowing and forced a lot of growing up quick. But we never butted heads, so to speak. She was never the daughter and I was never the father. We've always had this unique relationship of being equals and best friends." The otherworldly events that plagued Mike's life were never far from his mind but he somehow knew that she would be ok during infancy. Given all of his experiences and newborn daughter, it reminded me of another man's story that is similar to Mike's and I feel that it's worth a mention here.

Andrew's story began in 1968 at the age of ten years old. He went camping with his brother and father on Sebago Lake in Maine. During the night while everyone slept, Andrew was approached by three beings he did not recognize as human. The beings spoke to him telepathically and told him they were there to learn about him. He sensed an aggressiveness and was frightened by them. At one point, he felt paralyzed and was unable to move, though his mind wanted him to run. Andrew then remembered his brother in their tent and feared the beings might approach him, too. With that realization, he was able to move and ran to his brother's side. He could hear the beings outside the tent and tried to be as quiet as possible. They never approached further, so he assumed they had left. Andrew then said that morning had arrived in an instant, similar to Mike's UFO moving over the telephone pole. The "instant morning" seemed impossible to Andrew, and he had the feeling that more happened than what he remembered.

After that night, a lifetime of encounters occurred, most of them blurred, sparse memories of beings surrounding him, but he remembered nothing of any actual abduction scenarios. He did recall one night as an adult and after his daughter was born that they visited him one last time. During this encounter, they wanted to discuss Andrew's child, which upset him. He decided to stand his ground and refused their involvement with her. He reported that the visitations stopped after that conversation.

I asked Mike if he had made a similar declaration like Andrew had done. He said, "No, I didn't realize I had the power to...." Mike was struggling mentally with everything that was happening to him. While he knew his daughter was safe as a newborn, he eventually began to worry more about her and her brother (his then-fiancé's son). He continued, "I wasn't really into or versed on this stuff at the time but was emotionally drained and depressed at the fact that I was a walking plague and had cursed my kids, even though I knew it wasn't my fault." Mike shared with me that he thinks of that time in his life as "dark days". He could only really manage to get through one day at a time. Unfortunately, a little over a year after his daughter was born, another odd event took place.

The Creature in the Room

Mike was at home one evening while the rest of his family was out. He invited his neighbour over for some drinks and conversation, and while they sat and chatted, a ball of light entered the living room. He explained to me how the event unfolded: "The way the living room was set up at the time, where the couch was… there was two windows behind us. My neighbor was with me having a beer and just shootin' the shit. Like when I was a kid, a ball of light came over my shoulder, I assume it came in from the window or something and landed right at the base of the entertainment center, right at the bottom shelf. What appeared was a four and half, five-foot-tall, light-gray colored being. It looked like a grey alien with the big head and eyes. That's kinda all I can remember out of it. I don't remember anything else happening." For a little while, Mike had no memory of that encounter ever happening. Despite the loss of memory, something else would happen that would jog Mike's memory about the alien. He shared with me, "One day, the PS2 just stopped working. We sent it out to get it fixed. When we got it back, we put a disc in, and it still wouldn't work. I pulled another game off the shelf, and that one worked. That game was from the second shelf under the TV, the first game I tried was from the bottom shelf. I put in everything from that bottom shelf and nothing worked. It was weird, it's not that they just didn't work, it said, 'no data'. Every disc above that shelf worked just fine." A realization washed over Mike and the memory of the previous encounter came rushing back to him. I asked him if he brought it up to his neighbor, he said, "It never really came up, and it wasn't anything I was comfortable talking to him about either." I understood. Mike wasn't in a mental state to really handle or process what had been happening to him. He felt it was better to keep it within his family.

During this portion of the interview, when Mike

mentioned the alien, it reminded me of the 'Dover Demon' case out of Massachusetts. The story has fascinated me for years, and the little creature described by witnesses, in my opinion, seemed to have the earmarks of a grey alien. Though no UFO activity was reported in conjunction with the case, I wanted to research it for myself to see what camp this creature truly laid in: cryptozoology or ufology. I wasn't sure that I would uncover anything new, considering the case had been investigated thoroughly by legends in both otherworldly fields. I was determined, however, and committed to the research and dove in.

The Farm Street Creature
The first sighting of the creature occurred on April 21, 1977 when three seventeen-year-old boys were driving around their town of Dover, Massachusetts. As I refamiliarized myself with the account of witness Bill Bartlett, I was transported back to my time in high school, cruising the streets of Bar Harbor, Maine with my friends.

Growing up on Mount Desert Island may seem like a child's paradise, but the reality of it was dispiriting at first. The area is affluent, and when we moved to that beautiful, coastal hamlet in the late 1980s, it was obvious that we were outsiders. My parents were far from "well off" and we were treated as such, well, from my perspective. We moved a lot; the winters were brutal, and the summers crowded. My first summer on the island was spent attending a day camp at the elementary school, and with being the new kid, friends were hard to come by. I would spend my nights huddled around my boombox listening to Ice-T spin tales of a gangster lifestyle in the streets of Los Angeles; quite the contrast, I know. The hypnotic bass, made by producer Afrika Islam, helped my young mind escape into another world. But as the years went by, I grew to adore living by the ocean and ended up having a core group of close friends in high school. When I was seventeen, we spent almost every weekend night cruising the streets of Bar Harbor looking, I imagined, as cool as Ice-T must have been. In reality, we were simply driving around the four major streets of our town doing what we called "laps". As silly as it sounds, we enjoyed this pastime and often looked forward to it. We would communicate via CB radio, as this was before cellphones were the norm, and we'd talk to girls, smoke cigarettes and avoid the police. The Iceman would have been proud.

One night while doing laps, my friend and I noticed some odd lights floating down the Mount Desert Narrows, heading toward the pier and possibly beyond. We tracked the lights as we drove down West Street and then up Main Street, but with the many businesses obstructing our view, my friend suggested that we park down at Albert Meadow, by the shore path. As we pulled in, the lights had just come into view, and we walked close to the water's edge for a better look. We marveled at the sight as this giant, silent "thing" floated by us. We could see at least ten rows of lights from top to bottom. The last row of lights touched the water and we just couldn't figure out what this object was. We speculated that it was some sort of cruise ship, but with the lights touching the water, it didn't make sense. I suggested that it could be a UFO which was met with a shrug of my friend's shoulders and a sighed, "Maybe." We watched until it floated out of sight and finally called it a night. When I got home, I wrote down the experience, but ultimately didn't think any more about it. Until now, of course. Anyways….

I continued to read the Bartlett case; the following is a brief overview.

Cryptozoologist Loren Coleman firstly, and famously, investigated the case, even coining the term "Dover Demon". He then assembled a team of investigators – Joseph Nyman, Ed Fogg, and Walter Webb – to help facilitate timely interviews with witnesses. Bartlett's encounter was the first in a series of brief sightings of an odd creature.

It was late for a school night, 10:30pm, as the boys drove down Farm Street. Bartlett was behind the wheel and noticed an animal on top of a dilapidated stone wall on the side of the road. As the car approached, Bartlett got a better look at the animal and was awestruck at how odd it looked. In the book, *Monsters of Massachusetts: Mysterious Creatures of the Bay State*, Loren Coleman wrote, "Bartlett, who was behind the wheel of his 1971 Volkswagen Super Beetle, spotted something gingerly creeping along a low wall of loose stones on the left side of the road. At first, he thought it was a dog or a cat until his headlights hit the thing directly and he realized it was nothing he had ever seen before." The culmination of reports described the head of the creature as large and "figure eight" in shape. The neck was thin, and it had a distended torso, the arms and legs were described as "spindly". A hairless and grayish-colored skin was said to have a rough texture; similar to the skin described in one of Mike's encounters. Bartlett's sighting lasted mere moments, but knew he'd seen something strange. He asked his buddies if they saw what he had. They didn't, but saw how frightened Bartlett was and all agreed to turn around to see if they could find it again. The boys drove fast, and Bartlett's friends yelled from the vehicle, taunting whatever it was to show itself. It didn't, so the friends were dropped off and Bartlett went home. His father met him at the door and could see that he was upset and asked what had bothered him. Bartlett told the whole story and then drew a picture of the creature. The drawing was not the only one made that night.

Two hours later, around 12:30am, John Baxter was walking down Millers High Road after having left his girlfriend's house. About a mile into his walk he saw someone approaching him from the opposite direction (according to Coleman, this was 1.2 miles from Bartlett's encounter.) As John strained to see who it was, he thought it was a friend of his who lived on the street and called out to him. The figure stopped walking and just stared at John. He stopped walking as well and said, "Who is that?" There was no answer as the pair stood approximately twenty-five feet apart. John moved slightly causing the figure to run away. Coleman wrote, "…the figure scurried off to the left, running down a wooded gully and up the opposite bank." John's curiosity got the better of him and he followed the figure. Coleman continued, "John could see that it was some sort of creature. He saw it standing silhouette about thirty feet away. Its feet were 'molded' around the top of a rock several feet away from the tree. The creature was leaning toward the tree and had the long fingers of both hands entwined around the trunk, which was eight inches in diameter, as if for support." Baxter also created a sketch of the creature; it looked surprisingly similar to Bartlett's drawing.

The very next evening, a young woman named Abby Brabham was given a ride by a young man named Will Taintor. As they drove, Abby saw an odd creature on the side of the road. She described it as, "…it kind of looked a minute like an ape. And then I looked at the head and the head was very big and it was a very weird head. It had bright green eyes and the eyes just glowed like, they were just looking exactly at me." Taintor did not get as good a look at the creature but did confirm that a small, odd animal was on the side of the road. Abby made a sketch as well, and while crude, its head and eye shape were similar to the previous drawings.

Coleman and team interviewed all the witnesses within a week of their sightings and were impressed by the young men and woman on how they conducted themselves. Coleman, in an interview with *American Monsters,* stated, "The short story (no pun intended) is that over a two day period in April 1977, four people saw a small, 4 foot tall orange sharkskin creature (somewhat like Golem in Lord of the Rings) in three separate sightings, in Dover, Massachusetts, a rural location near Boston. The case goes down as unexplainable. I don't know the answer to 'what really happened' as all the eyewitnesses checked out and were found to be credible by law enforcement and other people in Dover."

The case, interestingly, does not end there. According to the website *Cryptopia,* after the Dover Demon story hit the news cycle, a man named Mark Sennot claimed to have possibly seen the creature five years prior in 1972 and stated, ''I don't know if we really saw something. We thought we did...we saw a small figure, deep in the woods, moving at the edge of the pond. We could see it moving in the headlights. We didn't know — it could have been an animal.'' Also, a year after the incident, Bartlett had another peculiar encounter one night. He was with his girlfriend, parked in a remote area when they heard something hit his car. He turned toward the noise and claimed to have seen a small being walking away from the car. He did not pursue it nor did he claim it to be the Dover Demon but found the encounter odd and worth mentioning.

In my search for any possible extraterrestrial connection to the case, I looked into UFO sightings in the Dover, Massachusetts area for April of 1977. I checked both MUFON and NUFORC databases which, not surprisingly, showed no reported UFO sightings. This included Dover and the surrounding areas, and I checked for the entire month of April 1977. I then accessed my personal library of cryptozoology books mentioning the case to see if there was anything I hadn't noticed or read before.

If you're in the camp of people who incessantly buy books before finishing the ones you already own, you'll have books on your shelf that you have been meaning to read but never cracked open. Such was the case for some of the books on my shelf, and one in particular covered the "Dover Demon" case. In

Curious Creatures of New England by Christopher Forest, he wrote of a Natick, Massachusetts family who witnessed a UFO during the EXACT timeframe of the demon sightings. It was reported that they also observed the creature on the night of April 21, 1977. Five members of the family were driving home from a dinner at their grandmother's when they briefly saw the creature. Oddly, the family did not think much of the incident and continued home.

The next day, one of the witnesses joked with the others that what they saw looked like an alien; the family was dismissive. Later that night, the family observed a light hovering in the sky above their vehicle, and it seemed to follow them for a while. Forest wrote of the encounter, "…there was a strange set of lights in the sky that night…. The lights then appeared to hover high in the sky over the car… and followed them all the way through the streets of Dover, into the streets of South Natick, through the streets of downtown Natick, and into West Natick. …the strange lights caused the family to pause and wonder exactly what they saw. Was it more than just a strange animal? There were no regular flight paths that would have caused a plane to take such a trip over the streets of Dover and Natick. It definitely appeared as if something weird was happening in the sky as well as the ground." Well, there it is! Finally, a UFO connection to the "Dover Demon" case. Unfortunately, it's the only source that I could find. I contacted Forest to see if he had any further information about the incident or the name of the family, but he has not returned my messages of inquiry.

If the UFO connection wasn't enough, in 2016 Loren Coleman wrote about a "men in black" encounter associated with the case in his *Cryptozoonews* blog. He wrote in part, "In the 1978 book I wrote with Jerome Clark, *Creatures of the Outer Edge*, I first documented my 1977 investigations of the Dover Demon. During my initial fieldwork, I coined the file name, 'Dover Demon', which found a life of its own. Importantly, I got to the case to examine all the eyewitness details before the media did. Now, almost 40 years later, searching the archives, retired Boston Museum of Science Planetarium assistant director Walt Webb forwarded a scan of an original article from 1977. The news item contains mention of a part of the Dover Demon episode I have never re-told – the weird Men in Black incident that happened in the wake of the Dover Demon sightings." Ooh, spooky! He continued, "The article was called *That 'Demon' in Dover was Real to UFO author in Needham* by Joan Wright." The article was published in two local papers, a day apart (*The Daily Transcript*, August 30, 1977 and *The Needham Chronicle*, August 31, 1977.) The article stated, "It could be coincidence, but Coleman implies it's more. He reported that two months to the day of the first sighting, two 'men in black' appeared at the Dover House (this is where Coleman worked at the time) looking for Coleman. A woman at the school gave the men Coleman's address, but they never contacted him. However, the men told the woman not to tell anyone about the Dover Demon. Wearing black leather jackets and white motorcycle helmets, the men, according to the woman, stood perfectly erect with their arms by their sides and spoke in a monotone. They identified themselves as investigators from National Geographic. Coleman spoke to a friend in Ohio who, in what appears to be another coincidence, experienced the same thing. The man said that three years ago, after a sighting in Ohio, two men fitting the same description, talking the same way, and also identifying themselves as being from National Geographic, demanded of some witnesses that they not say a word about what they saw."

I was happy to have finally found some sort of extraterrestrial connection to the "Dover Demon" case, and I wanted to continue researching the Natick family, but that could wait. Mike's story is far from over.

Brilliant Light

Mike's lifelong love of all thing's nature had transferred to his family. The summer that followed his living room alien incident, they travelled to White Lake State Park in Tamworth, New Hampshire. That body of water was formed glacially and continues to be a beautiful summer destination. The *New Hampshire State Park* website stated, "During the Ice Age, glacial ice was buried beneath glacial till or debris. When the ice melted, a depression was created which gradually filled with water." While their camping trip was uneventful, extraterrestrially speaking, there was an innocuous moment that caught Mike's attention. He told me, "We had gone up camping and my wife, at the time, ended up with these three strange little dots that made a triangle and I was like, 'Wow, that's weird' and she said, 'it's just mosquito bites, don't worry about it.'" A large number of alien abductees have reported waking up with strange markings on their body after an encounter. While the types of markings vary widely, one common marking is that of three dots in the form of a triangle. This particular sign in mathematics is called a "therefore sign" and looks like this (∴) minus the parentheses. In regard to alien abduction, it has been associated as "trace evidence" of having been taken. The website *UFO Insight* wrote of the markings, "Typically, the day after their abduction, they'll notice marks — which may or may not feel sore — that they can't explain; they've no knowledge of how they acquired them. Typical are bruises believed to have been left by restraints applied by their abductors to stop them moving whilst undergoing procedures. Also typical are puncture marks thought to be caused by needles, often in a triangular formation — like a bite from a three-fanged snake — and groups of marks arranged in a grid or geometric pattern." For Mike, he associated the markings on his wife as a potential sign of some sort of alien intervention. Having not remembered any further incidents, he tried to forget about it.

As a vacation destination, Mike and his family enjoyed the site at White Lake and planned another trip for the following summer. He told me, "So, we got the same site and we had a bunch of new tents, gear and stuff. I wanna say, the second day in, on the same spot, three little red dots appeared on her again." This time, his wife wasn't so dismissive, and Mike couldn't shake the feeling that it meant something. Later on, this sparked a memory of another occurrence during that same trip. While he and his ex-wife shared the memory, he's not entirely sure it was real and thought it might be just a dream. He explained, "It's kinda hazy so I don't want to sell it as the truth, but we both remember somebody pulling into the campsite in the middle of the night. Brilliant headlights, just shining into our campsite. I was annoyed at the time, like, 'What the fuck, they must be from Massachusetts!'" Mike and I shared a laugh at this comment. He continued, "I kinda had this weird vision of unzipping the tent and sticking my head out to see what was going on. We had the tent and we also had this screen porch that we put around the picnic table and coolers of food, ya know? I remember there was no wind that night but when I stuck my head out, there's this bright light but it's really windy, just within our area. Like this cyclone of wind, I don't remember seeing anything or feeling anything, but it all felt off somehow. I don't know how to explain it." I asked him if anything else happened, he said, "No, I just went back in the tent and zipped it up." The implication here is that with Mike's "off feeling", perhaps it was more than a family from the city barreling up to White Lake in the middle of the night. The wind confused him, and he had trouble articulating its description. Can't say I blame him. I think it would be safe to add this occurrence to Mike's continued encounters with the strange, whether a dream or not.

Boxes in the Snow

A few years later, Mike found himself in the most curious of landscapes. He explained to me, "I don't necessarily remember how it started. I don't remember waking up with lights in the sky or in the bedroom or anything like that. It just kinda started 'in scene'. I was on this landscape that I didn't recognize. It kinda looked like I was in a desert, but everything was white, and the sand wasn't quite sand. There were two or three beings behind me; I was walking of my own free will, but it kinda seemed like I was being led, too. The only thing you could see in this landscape, other than this big, white desert, was these little bunkers that went into the ground." Mike said that the bunkers were about the size and shape of a dumpster and were scattered about at random. He continued, "They tell me to dig in this soil, for lack of a better term, I'm not quite sure what to call it because it's not really sand. And it had this crunchy layer on top, like you know how snow gets that way sometimes? Anyways, I'm digging with my hands, and after you get through that crunchy layer, it's very fine and as I pulled a handful up it would fill back in. It was cool, too, not cold like snow but kinda like beach sand after you dig down a little. They had me do that for a while and I had no idea why." Mike was digging and digging and confused about what was happening. After some time, they told him to stop and that he needed to look up into the sky. He said, "Similar to the face in the window from when I was a kid, there's this giant face in the horizon. All I can see is this white landscape and this black background on the horizon, no stars or anything. So, there's this black backdrop with this giant face that filled a good part of the horizon and it feels like that's why I'm supposed to be there. I then get this imagery in my head of a lot of nature scenes, oceans, volcanos and then it evolves into this chaotic destruction of earth.

My overall impression is it had to do with how we treat the earth or that it wasn't going to last, something like that."

The imagery that Mike described has been shared by many experiencers. They have spoken about humanity's involvement in the earth's demise, natural disasters, and the ultimate destruction of earth. John E. Mack, through his studies, developed a theory about why people may be having those images shown to them. The *Nova* documentary series interviewed Mack who said of the concept, "…in a number of abductees — not just people I see, but the ones Budd Hopkins and other people see — is to produce some kind of new species to bring us together to produce a hybrid species which — the abductees are sometimes told — will populate the earth or will be there to carry evolution forward after the human race has completed what it is now doing, namely the destruction of the earth as a living system."

"All of that just ends," Mike continued, "and now I'm at the foot of the driveway at the Farmington house and I'm led up the driveway by these two beings. They're about five-foot-tall and have that typical grey alien face that we're all accustomed to but they're a kinda dark brown. You don't hear many reports of aliens talking to each other but, on this occasion, I heard one of them say to the other, 'Don't let him turn around.' Of course, when you hear that, in any situation, you turn around." We shared another chuckle. Mike continued, "I looked back towards the road and by this tree I see this six-foot creature with eyes like a cat. It looked similar to the *Creature from the Black Lagoon* but all black, not scaly or anything and it peered at me from around the tree. That's the last thing I remember." Mike advised that he investigated the area the next day for any signs of the beings having been there, he did not find anything out of the ordinary.

Pulled Over by Extraterrestrials
"Well, that's just as weird as anything else." I said to Mike after he told me that last story. He responded with, "Well good, I'm glad I'm staying on track." We both burst out with laughter, and he added, "Oh, another weird thing around that time was when my truck pulled itself over." You would think that nothing would surprise me at this point, but it did. Mike continued, "I was in the truck, it was night and I was driving; I think I was in Milton, New Hampshire. On my left, there's kinda like a stone cliff where they blasted out the granite to put the road in. On the passenger side is the lake, and there is this light over the water. As I got a little bit closer, the light is getting bigger, and I realize that it's some sort of craft or object. I started to get nervous and worked up and was like, 'Not today!' and I sped up. I see a spot where I thought I could turn around, at this point, it would be worth crashing the car. Anyway, I banged a 'u-ey' as quick as I could and started going back the opposite way. I couldn't see the light anymore and thought I had gotten away from it, and that's when the cab of the truck filled up with this blue light and the truck came to a stop." Mike explained to me the surrealness of that moment. Everything was still, quiet, and haunting. He said he felt like the truck was on ice or thought that he might be floating. Also, it

reminded me of the scene from *Close Encounters of the Third Kind* when Richard Dreyfuss' character, Roy, had pulled over his work truck to check a map when strange things began to happen. Not to wander away, Mike added, "The truck pulled itself over horizontally, not like I pulled in, but the truck just slid to the side of the road. I was obviously terrified, and I was locked up and couldn't move my head or arms. The only thing I could move was my foot and I hit the gas and I could hear the truck rev up, but I didn't go anywhere. I blacked out after that." I asked Mike if he remembered waking up in the truck or anything else after blacking out, he said, "No, and I really don't have any reason why I would have been in that area, at night, during that time. All I can think of is that I needed to be in that area so that could happen, or something, I don't know."

Brokedown Palace

Toward the end of 2005, Mike experienced an event that would truly rock his mental foundation. It started when he and his family moved down the road from his parents' home in Farmington. They had barely settled into the house when Mike awoke one night and walked out of his bedroom and out the front door. He explained, "My wife, at the time, and I had gone to bed. At some point in the night, I apparently had gotten dressed and walked to my old house in Farmington, the green house. I was by the corner of the house just standing there, I don't know why I was standing there, like I was waiting for something. I remember pulling cough drops out of the front pocket of my shirt and just eating them, killing time, like I'm waiting for a bus or something." I snickered at the thought and kept typing. Mike continued, "Eventually I got bored and walked down toward the front of the house where the door was. As I walked around to do that, from the left front corner, I see this white ball of light, like basketball-sized light and it's about 2 or 3 feet off the ground." I stopped typing and closed my eyes. In my mind, I was in front of this house. Mike isn't there, but I'm seeing everything from his perspective. He's drawn me into another encounter; I'm scared and looking at this basketball-sized light. Mike's voice resumes, "As soon as I make contact with it, like eye contact with it, it starts approaching me very quickly. As it's approaching, it's also rising in height. As it got closer to me and rising in height, when it was around shoulder level, my mind said, this is a big white dog and it's about to pounce on you." The sudden change to the white dog scared me. I could feel my face emoting fear, I had raised eyebrows, a taut brow, and a half-opened mouth. I realized I was typing and as I continued to do so, Mike said, "So, I closed my eyes and turned away and braced for this dog to hit me. I waited a few seconds and there's no impact. I opened my eyes to see what was going on and that's when I found myself engulfed in this bright blue light and realized I was like 15-20 feet off the ground. I didn't see a craft or anything, next thing I know, I woke up in bed screaming." I'm watching this as a horror movie now. I'm still scared, but it's for Mike. I've had some strange encounters over the years, but what Mike has been experiencing is nothing short of a nightmare.

    I went back into author mode and asked, "When

you woke up in bed screaming, do you remember your wife trying to calm you down or anything like that at all?"

He said, "This happened quite a bit when I was living there. We coined the phrase 'window ninjas'. It was for when the wind would hit the window just right and it would make this little whistle and it'd catch you off guard. So, when I would wake up in bed screaming, because it happened so often, she would say, 'Window ninja?' I'd say, 'Yeah.' And we would go back to bed and kind of ignore it. After this particular incident, I didn't talk to her. We didn't talk for like three days. I finally approached her and told her what happened, and she was like, 'That's so weird, I remember you getting out of bed fully dressed.'" This confused Mike. He explained to me that he never went to bed fully dressed. He thinks that he got up at an earlier point during the night, got dressed, and went back to bed.

I mentioned earlier that Mike was in a difficult mental place. This continued for some time and it started to affect his marriage. He started to reveal more layers of his life to me and intimately shared, "This is also around the time it started getting rocky for us. I remember getting pissed at her. She was telling me nonchalantly that she remembered me getting out of bed fully dressed and never stopped me. I told her, 'this whole thing is your fucking fault.' Which wasn't fair, it wasn't her fault. I know that now, but at the time I was upset, and I didn't talk to her again for like another day and a half. Once I got over my little fit, I brought it back up again to get her side of what happened. She said, 'I don't remember you getting out of bed, dressed, in the middle of the night.' I was like, 'What? We had a conversation about this a day ago.' She said, 'I don't know what you're talking about, I don't remember any conversation about this.' And that was a crucial blow to me. Like, I was thinking, did we have this conversation? In some of the research I have done, I have read where they [aliens] will block your partner's memory of things, too. But I wasn't really thinking about that at the time. I was just so confused about everything." Mike knew something had to change but he didn't know what to do.

At this point in our conversation, my mind wandered to the movie, *The Blair Witch Project,* and I felt like the character of Josh. In the movie, Josh's gear had been thrown about and there was a jelly-like substance over a lot of his belongings. Another character, Heather is capturing everything on camera, and they're all scared. Mike (the third lead character in the movie) and Josh are begging her to stop filming but she refused. There's a jump cut to where she's finally packing up and Josh is filming and says to her, "I see why you like this video camera so much. It's not quite reality." I felt this way, despite being transported into some of his moments, because those are not my moments. It's scary, I feel empathy for him, but none of it is mine and I'm seeing it all through a lens. It's easy to write about another person's story and I only wish I could take away some of the fear for him; I can't. I wish he could take the metaphorical camera and look through the view finder so he could just have a moment of relief, as Heather and Josh experienced. Mike knew something had to change but was unsure of what to do. That's when the early beginnings of his research started but he lacked focus.

Soon after that experience, Mike's wife encouraged him to see a doctor. He was uncomfortable with the notion but knew he should at least try. He shared, "I started going through basically, not a full mental breakdown, but it was like, an everything-I-have-ever-known type of breakdown. I go to the doctor, he's like, 'So, what's wrong with you?' I said, 'Nothing!' He said, 'Well, why are you here?' I'm like, 'My wife brought me!' He kinda sighed and said, 'Ok, well, why did your wife bring you?'" I couldn't help but snicker at the exchange and Mike did, too. He continued, "I didn't tell him the full truth with all the UFO shit, whatever, but I told him a version of it. I said, 'I'm starting to see things out of the corner of my eye. I know it's not there, but I can't help notice it.' After he finished the examination he just said, 'Alright, you have anxiety.' He throws me on some anti-anxiety shit; Chantix, I think. It rocked my stomach; I couldn't take it and it wasn't actually helping me. It just made me want to puke all the time. There was just so much happening. I was seeing aliens everywhere. I'd walk into a room and I'd see an alien sitting in a rocking chair and we didn't even own a rocking chair! I'm thinking this is my mind breaking down. I couldn't even go outside when it was dark. I used to have to leave for work at like five in the morning and it was pitch black outside. I used to park my vehicle right by the front porch and it was still too far away. It was like ten steps, but there was this panicked, mad dash to get into the truck. I called out of work a lot because the way I had to drive there took me down this route, up this hill and there would be this bright light in the sky and I was terrified that it was a UFO. I know now that it was the Sirius star but back then, I'd get to that area and whip the truck around, I'd call out of work because I could not drive past the thing. This is my state of mind at this point."

This whole part of the conversation felt frenzied, he was talking fast, and seemed like he may be feeling those emotions again. I wanted to give him Heather's camera, but it turned out that he didn't need it. Soon after his visit to the doctor, he got a house call from an extraterrestrial. After that night, everything changed.

Communion

Mike told me about another "troll" creature that visited him. While relating the story, he spoke with more confidence than I'd heard before, perhaps foreshadowing the change that was about to take place. He shared with me, "I'm lying there in bed and this troll looking thing… similar to the trolls I saw when I was younger, but this one was bigger. He's got these big black eyes. He shows up with this toolbox. I actually feel like this is a screen memory, for what it's worth. During this time actually, I was finally really looking into everything, aliens and all that, trying to understand what was happening." Mike was at his breaking a point and wanted to address all that had happened and truly wanted everything to stop. That's when the serious research began. He read books, studied people's encounters and talked to witnesses. He tried to learn everything he could about the phenomena. During his research, he found that a lot of experiencers believed that there were both good and bad aliens. Mike vehemently disagreed, and told me, "I read some stuff about good aliens and bad aliens and I think it's bullshit. This thing, this plague, has scarred me for life. People can fuck off with all that."

As you've read, he's had a lot of different types of encounters and he seemed steadfast in this belief. Again, I really can't blame the guy. He never knows when the next encounter is going to happen, and he's mostly left with memory loss and confusion. Mike moved on and continued discussing the encounter. He said, "Anyways, he's next to my bed and he's got this toolbox and he's tinkering with the top of my head." I stopped typing just to process that statement. Mike didn't miss a beat and continued with, "I ended up playing 20 questions with him, which he did not seem impressed with at all. I'm asking, 'Why are you here? What is this? What is that?' I'm not getting real answers from him. It's almost like the guy is there to fix your water heater." We shared another laugh. He resumed saying, "He just doesn't care what I'm saying to him, he's just there to work. Whether spiritual, emotional, I don't know how to put it, but it was like a rewiring of my brain. He kinda put me in this spot to where I could accept what was happening. That this was real, this is happening, I wasn't crazy. To me, this was a rewiring. The terminology that he used with me about what he was doing was, 'I'm just doing some tinkering.' The reason I think this is a screen memory, the impression I get now, is that this was a visual representation of what occurred, but not what actually occurred. Like, it was a way for them to show me how they helped me with acceptance."

I was in awe of his realization, whether any of this was true or not, Mike had finally gotten himself to the point of acceptance. That is something many people struggle with, trauma or not. And he got there. Was it because of extraterrestrial intervention? I cannot answer that. Mike would admit that he couldn't either. And that's ok. Perception is reality. This is happening to him because this is what the man is experiencing and for everything that he's been through, the scars, the failing marriage, the trauma of it all; he now has acceptance. I don't care how he got there, I'm just glad that he did.

Stranger Things
(2010-2015)

In July of 2011, the New Hampshire State Division of Historical Resources erected a historical marker at the site of Betty and Barney Hill's abduction and Mike was the catalyst. We have discussed the marker on a few occasions, and I visited the area before it had been erected. For the purposes of this writing and for my own personal enjoyment, I have since gone back out there for the obligatory picture, which is in this book. *New Hampshire Public Radio* interviewed Mike about the marker and wrote on their website, "Their story lives on in the form of a historical marker along Route 3 in Lincoln. The state put up the marker in 2011, fifty years after the events reportedly occurred. As part of our ongoing series,

'Marking History,' NHPR's Michael Brindley met with Mike Stevens of Farmington, who led the effort to get the marker put up. Stevens says while skeptics have come up with a number of theories debunking the Hill's claims, he's a believer."

After Mike started the campaign, Kathleen Marden joined the cause. She wrote an article about it for the *Open Minds* website and wrote in part, "Several years ago, Mike Stevens, a Farmington, NH, man circulated a petition to request a marker to commemorate Betty and Barney Hills' UFO experience. The State of NH Division of Historical Resources, Department of Cultural Resources advised him that a formal request would be required. I, as the Hills' niece and trustee of Betty's estate, then worked with the state over the next 3-4 years to complete the process. Employees at the Department of Cultural Resources called upon me to suggest appropriate text for the marker—a challenge in and of itself. Every statement had to be footnoted and supported by ample evidence that it was true and accurate. In all, the wording for the 12-line plaque had 20 footnotes and 28 sources listed in its bibliography."

Signs of Life

In my sit down with Mike, we discussed his behind-the-scenes thought process about the marker and why he pursued such an endeavor. He told me, "I had a bone spur in my ankle that was shredding my Achilles tendon. I knew I was going to be couch bound so I bought Marden's book, *Captured!* I'm sitting there on the couch, eating pain pills and reading the book. I got into a bunch of paranormal shows and got this idea that there should be a historical marker for Betty and Barney. I didn't really think I would ever actually get it but thought this was a good way to piss off people in high places." Through our personal discussions and from statements like this, I could infer that Mike may have some issues with people in authority, societal norms and the like. A lot of us do, however, this could be interpreted as a sign of Oppositional Defiant Disorder (ODD). I actually had no idea that this was even a thing until I researched "issues with figures of authority". The *American Academy of Family Physicians* websites stated, "ODD is often comorbid with attention-deficit/hyperactivity disorder, conduct disorder, and mood disorders, including anxiety and depression." Also, "Adults and adolescents with a history of ODD have a greater than 90% chance of being diagnosed with another mental illness in their lifetime. They are at high risk of developing social and emotional problems as adults, including suicide and substance use disorders." Despite everything with his mental health, anxiety pills, pain pills, finding acceptance, and more, it's all a work in progress and Mike still had a life to live and continued plans with the marker.

    When he was first getting started with the process, he wasn't quite sure how to go about it. His wife, at the time, encouraged him to get a computer and that it could open up some new possibilities for him. Mike was a self-proclaimed "technical dumb-dumb" and was apprehensive in obtaining a computer. He said, "I was always a woodsy guy and never needed a laptop or computer." He told me that he was eventually tricked into getting one through his love of nature. He shared, "My wife knew that I loved taking pictures out in nature and I would use those disposable 35mm film cameras. She bought a computer and a digital camera and told me, 'Surprise, here's a digital camera! But you need the computer to download the pictures.' I was just dumb enough to start learning how to use everything." I had a belly laugh at the comment. He continued, "So, I started emailing people like Kathleen Marden and Bill Barnes of *UFO Magazine* and was like, 'Hey, I'm trying to get a marker, will you support it?' At the same time, I have no idea what the process is to get a marker. I was even giving out my senator's email address and telling people to contact them and to tell them we need it. I had no idea it had to go through the Historical Resource department. So, it was a bit of a shit-show, and it's a miracle that it even happened." Through the process, he met Andy Kitt.

Andy Kitt, who founded the KRI Center for Consciousness Studies and the Seacoast Paranormal Research Group, played a small role in the petition. Mike said, "I was a part of KRI, and I joined Andy's Seacoast Paranormal Research Group and thought they would be a good place to start finding signatures for the marker petition." While Mike was navigating through the new, wonderous world of the internet, he contacted Andy via email and through the website, *MeetUp.com.* Mike isn't the world's classiest writer and was a bit crass in his communication with Andy. When Mike started electronically interacting with the groups, he rubbed Andy the wrong way with some of the ufological pictures he posted and thought Mike wouldn't be around long. Mike said, "He came at me hard during that time. I was using copyrighted pictures, but I had no idea what I was doing, and I think he thought I'd just go away." Mike finally met Andy when he showed up for one of the group's in-person meetings. Mike said of the meeting, "The only fucking reason I showed up to my first meeting was the way he had phrased the meeting topics. It was like, 'Oh, and there might be a petition to sign if Mike Stevens actually shows up.' So, that was my cue to show up and shove it down his fucking throat." All of this is tongue-in-cheek and said in as positive a way as possible because Mike and Andy have since become great friends. Mike said, "It's not the prettiest of stories but that's how it began."

"Might not be pretty," I said, "but it turned into something pretty cool." Mike agreed.

Before KRI's inception, Mike, Andy, and others started making plans to form a new group focused on helping those in the community afflicted or dealing with some aspect of the paranormal. Mike rarely discussed the details of his encounters with outsiders and knew the inner turmoil that it can create so he wanted to explore helping others like him. To accomplish this, he knew that he had to open up to the group more. He and future members of KRI met one evening to discuss plans of its creation; no one was prepared for what transpired that night.

Mike shared, "This was before KRI, but we were SPRG and a few of us went to the Coat of Arms in Portsmouth, New Hampshire to discuss plans on creating KRI. They knew I had some UFO experiences, but they didn't know any of the details. They were asking me a bunch of questions; pun intended, they were probing me." I couldn't help but snicker and so did Mike. "After a while," he continued, "one of the members there, a psychic/medium, got this image of something, like… holy shit it scared her. She's used to seeing dead people at this point, that's old hat for her, but she sees this creature in front of her and the three of us are just staring at her. She's making these weird faces and we don't really know what the fuck is going on, and then she starts to describe it. She said that she was seeing this big six or seven foot being and said that the thing was nasty and that she didn't like it. She was telling us that this thing doesn't want me to talk about it in fact, it said, 'He's not going to talk about it, this conversation is done.' She's dealt with spirits before, so she kinda pushes it and thinks, 'I make the rules here.' As this is going on, the rest of us felt a palpable change in the atmosphere. The air changed and it had this sticky, gross feeling to it. After she was done with it, it all went away. We stopped the conversation about it, and everything went back to normal. The reason I'm sharing this story is because, to me, personally, I finally felt like somebody believed me for the first time, because she could see it." An instantaneous smile formed on my face; I was elated for Mike. I excitedly asked, "Did you tell her that?!"

"Not at the time," he said, "but over the years, as we became close, I eventually told her." I said to Mike, "Wow, finally some validation after like thirty years." He sighed heavily, hinting at his disheartenment with the extraterrestrial phenomena. The abuse and trauma that he's endured over the years hid inside him, but at that moment, in that pub in Portsmouth, someone saw a small piece of it, and he was relieved. Notwithstanding, he said, "Even after that experience, I don't think she quite knew what to do with it."

Dr. Dolittle and April Foolishness

The appearance of animals in extraterrestrial contact has been reported on numerous occasions. Whitley Strieber, an experiencer and author, wrote in his book, *Communion*, of a barn owl that he would see outside his window at night and would recall dreams of an alien abduction the following day. An excerpt reads, "I awoke the morning of the twenty-seventh very much as usual, but grappling with a distinct sense of unease and a very improbable but intense memory of seeing a barn owl staring at me through the window sometime during the night. I remember how I felt in the gathering evening of the twenty-seventh, when I looked out onto the roof and saw that there were no owl tracks in the snow. I knew I had not seen an owl. I shuddered, suddenly cold, and drew back from the window, withdrawing from the night that was falling so swiftly in the woods beyond. But I wanted desperately to believe in that owl." Another experiencer and author, Mike Clelland, wrote of owls in his encounters, as well. Owl symbolism has been connected to wisdom and mysterious events and one of Clelland's experiences was with three owls; they flew above him while he camped. Experiencers have spoken of oversized raccoons, albino deer, and many more that would appear outside and sometimes inside their homes and often preceding an abduction event. Mike has seen them, too.

Near the wildlife refuge in New Hampshire that borders Pease Air National Guard, Mike encountered animals on multiple occasions while strange lights moved erratically in the skies above him. He said to me, "I used to travel that route quite a bit and often late at night when I would leave the Center. The whole area has a creepy feel to it and it's a dark road, not a lot of streetlights. I go through there one night, I get to a stop sign, and you can only go right or left, straight is a driveway. I'm at that stop sign and, in this driveway, there were two deer, but they were albino, I mean like pure white." I am in no way an expert on New Hampshire wildlife, but albino deer did not sound right to me. I've lived in New England my entire life and while I've heard of white deer, I've never seen one myself, nor has anyone I know told me that they have observed one. Also, do not confuse this with "white-tailed deer", which are common. I won't, however, base my opinion on that limited knowledge so I researched albino deer in the state of New Hampshire. I found that, if observed, people typically report what is called a "piebald deer". This type of deer varies in color and has white splotches throughout its hide. According to the *New Hampshire Fish and Game* website, the piebald is rare, appearing about 1 in 30,000. A true albino deer is different, and according to a *WMUR* interview, Fish and Game employee Daniel Bergeron advised, "The piebald condition is different from true albinism, which is even more rare. True albino deer lack pigment and have pink eyes and white hooves." That does clarify things a bit. Mike added, "It's not impossible that they were albino deer, but it was a weird situation."

Another albino animal encounter that Mike experienced included an owl. He stated, "Right down the road from there, closer to the base, out of the blue, this huge white owl just drops out of nowhere, in front of the car and spreads its wings out. The wings went from one side of the car to the other, like driver to passenger side." I also researched white owls in the New Hampshire area and the closest species that I could find was the snowy owl. According to the *New Hampshire Fish and Game* website, there is "No data for NH. Population trend is unknown." And that they are a "Rare and irregular winter visitor throughout NH…." The site stated about their size and color: "Up to 28" long and up to 57" wingspan. Body color is white with dark bars and spots. Females and young have more markings; males have markings when they are young but tend to lose them and become whiter as they age." It is certainly possible that Mike observed a snowy owl and readily admits that, but it's the strangeness of the situation that stayed with Mike. He's observed lights in the sky in that area, even on the same road that he saw the owl. The implication is that the owl and deer could be screen memories. At this point in Mike's life, he's learned to follow his intuition, and these animal sightings felt strange to him.

Another night, while in that area, Mike observed "…a plasma ball, it wasn't quite a light or even an object and it was like 25-30 feet in length, kinda football shaped. I did the same thing as the night in Milton and was like, 'Not today!' and whipped the car around. I was like, 'What am I doing? I just need to face this stuff.' So, I whipped the car around again and back to the area. There's this build up, and I was like 'Shit!' I had like four cigarettes in this one-mile stretch, and I'm about to reach where it was, and it's not there." Relief washed over him, and he said, "Alright, this is good." That feeling, unfortunately, would not last long. He continued, "I keep driving, near where I saw the deer and I look out the driver side window. There's a couple houses, kinda scattered, there's an old farm and there's this big field with a tree line behind it… and I see the object again. I pick up speed a little bit and I'm trying to get to this corner so I can see it from another angle. When I got around the corner, it was still there, it didn't do anything. I'm in Newington at that point and I made it back to Farmington without anything happening." I'm happy for Mike in this moment. He made a decision to face his fear and it worked out in this particular instance. The strange albino animal encounters, unfortunately, continued.

A year or so after the Betty and Barney Hill marker was put up, Mike's marriage had completely fallen apart and he had moved in with his brother in Somersworth, New Hampshire. It would seem that no matter where Mike lived, strange events would follow him. He shared with me, "When I was living there, I couldn't smoke in the house, no big deal, but he did have a little porch I could go out on. So, I had this routine where I'd come down in the morning, make my cup of coffee, put my boots on, and go out on that porch for a cigarette. I'm sitting out there one morning, it's like 5am, having my first smoke of the day and I look out toward the street and see this little creature. The top half of it looked like a mink or some type of weasel. It was pure white and had these big black eyes similar to the Greys. It fattened out toward the bottom, kinda like a cat and the tail was fluffy like a raccoon's tail with light tan rings toward the end of it. The thing walked up, sat down, and started staring at me. I stared at it for a little bit and said out loud to it, 'I don't know what the hell you are but you're freaking me out and it's too early for this shit.' And as soon as I said that, it got up and walked away. I then felt like a complete asshole. Like shit, it understood. I should have asked it some questions." We laughed again, and while a harmless encounter, Mike thought this could have been associated with extraterrestrials. I looked into weasel wildlife native to New Hampshire and found some interesting information. The *New Hampshire Fish and Wildlife* website states, "New Hampshire has weasels in abundance. In fact, there are six members of the Mustelidae, or weasel family. They include (from smallest to largest): ermine (also known as the short-tailed weasel), long-tailed weasel, pine marten, mink, fisher and river otter. All of these, except the marten, are common to abundant throughout most of New Hampshire, but most of us can count on our hands the number of times we have seen any one of them. They may be abundant, but are scarce to our view. Two species, the ermine and long-tailed weasel, disappear nearly completely in winter by turning white as snow!" For the sake of sticking with attention to detail and authenticity, Mike's encounter happened during the summer and in a well populated, residential area. In regard to their tails, I found that long-tailed weasels do have a fluffy tail similar to a raccoon. However, I could find no instance in which an animal from the weasel family had rings on their tails, and along with that, none fattened out toward the bottom as Mike described. Also, their eyes are small and differ quite a bit from Mike's description. What are we to make of it? Much like every other encounter, I have no idea.

Another event happened during Mike's tenure at his brother's home. He shared with me, "I had this little camera that I could plug into my TV and I would point it out the window to see the moon and watch the sky. One night, I was watching and saw something; this little blip on the screen. It freaked me out though, so I called my ex-wife. I had no one else to call and I'm freaking out, so I'm talking to her. She said this phrase that stuck with me, she said, 'April is always hard for you.' I asked her what she meant; she didn't know."

When I heard that statement, "April is always hard for you," I immediately thought of John Keel's book, *The Mothman Prophecies*, and specifically the chapter, "Purple Lights and April Foolishness." In that chapter, Keel described a UFO encounter that seems like a mishmash of a lot of Mike's sightings and feelings. An excerpt stated, "One hour later, at 1:35am on April 3, 1967, I had my best sighting. A clearly defined circular object suddenly zipped down from the sky and passed parallel to my car. It was so colorful, that it was burned into my memory. The greenish upper surface was topped by a bright red light. There were reddish "portholes" or circular lights around the rim. The colors were so brilliant they were almost unearthly. It disappeared behind some trees to my left. I felt it was very close … perhaps only a few hundred feet from my car." And, "First of all, although I am used to prowling graveyards and TNT areas alone late at night, I was scared to death." Despite his fear, Keel never stopped searching for the truth and neither did Mike.

Phone Home

A little while after Mike's brief sighting with his camera and TV setup, an encounter of levity occurred. He shared, "I was lying in bed and there was this little alien, 3-4 foot tall and kinda E.T. like. I say E.T., like the movie creature, because it had a t-shirt on!" I had one of those moments again where I stopped typing. Just needing a moment to process his statement. We both laughed and Mike joked, "He must have gotten into my clothes!" Because of the ridiculousness of what he witnessed, he assumed that it was another screen memory. He continued with the story, "I look over at him and I was just like, 'Fuck it. I'm done fighting', and I reached out my hand to him. I said, 'Let's just go, let's just do this. Let's do this peacefully.' He grabs my hand and we're walking down the stairs, more like a ladder cause I'm in the attic, and we're just about to reach the stairs to the first floor and I said, 'I'm going to get to remember this time, right?' He didn't speak to me telepathically, it was with his mouth, and he said, 'You can see this?' And I was like, 'Yeah, am I going to get to remember this time?' The next thing I know, everything goes black and I just wake up the next morning."

Time after time during this interview, Mike has shared something so strange with me that you'd think I'd become desensitized to it, I wasn't. I'm especially astonished by all these creatures. While humorous, I don't think I would have been as easy going as Mike was. I get it, though. He wasn't apathetic either, he had interest, but this was his life, and he wanted answers. In regard to the alien itself, he most associated it with E.T. because of the t-shirt. Besides the movie, *E.T. the Extra-Terrestrial,* the species was also featured in *Star Wars: Episode I – The Phantom Menace.* According to the *Wookieepedia, Star Wars Fandom* website, the E.T. character is part of the "Asogians" species and, "were paddle-footed, large-eyed sentients indigenous to Brodo Asogi." According to alien abductees and experiencers, in our world, there's no one species that meets all the criteria for Mike's description. This is why he thought it may be another screen memory and perhaps an attempt to make the encounter easier on him. And maybe that's how some of that "tinkering" from his previous encounter was supposed to help him.

Premonitions in the Sky with Diamonds

Mike had another bizarre event occur during this same timeframe and admitted that it may have been a dream. He told me, "I was in bed, I looked out the window and saw a light. I got up to look at it and there's this diamond shaped object, kinda spinning very slowly right outside the window. It looks fake, it looks like metal and rivets, it looks industrial almost. And it's painted yellow, like a school bus. And then, as it spins, it has a window, a square window. As that window spins to me directly I remember being in this room, it looked like a basement. You can see pipes and stuff, nothing space age. The next day for work, we have to work in this old school, it's not in session and it's just me and my boss there. My boss needed to leave to get something and left me there. All of a sudden, I'm stuck in this antique school and I don't know if that was a premonition, but the basement of the school looked like that UFO and I was scared. I did my work as fast I could and got the fuck out of there."

There have been reports of increased paranormal and psychic ability during and after extraterrestrial encounters. The *UFO Insight* website states, "In a 2012 study by Kathleen Marden and Denise Stoner, both experienced UFO researchers and abduction investigators, the connections between psychic or paranormal ability and alien contact were interesting, to say the least. Although they would only study seventy-five cases, the indications are that some kind of new or increased psychic ability takes place. 88% of those in the study would report increased paranormal activity in their homes following such incidents, with just over half indicating this paranormal activity had not happened before their encounters. 79% would also indicate a new 'psychic' ability that they were not aware of before." I guess we can add "dream premonitions" to Mike's already long list of what he calls "weird shit."

If the person reading this is anything like me, when Mike described the UFO as "diamond shaped", their mind conjured the "Cash-Landrum Incident" from 1980. It's a fascinating case and the following is a brief overview. On December 29, 1980, at around

9pm, Betty Cash, Vickie Landrum, and Colby Landrum (Vickie's grandson) were driving on Texas back roads through dense woods. They all saw some sort of light above the trees and assumed it was an airplane approaching the Houston Airport. A moment later, while coming out of a curve in the road, the witnesses saw a large diamond-shaped object hovering at treetop level expelling flames and significant heat from its bottom. In an interview conducted at Bergstrom Air Force Base by Captain John Camp, Acting Staff Judge Advocate, Captain Terry Davis, Claims Officer, and Miss Pat Wolf, Assistant Claims Officer, Betty Cash said in part, "…after we got through eating, we got in the car and started home, and we drove approximately... I'd say maybe twelve miles, when we spotted this object, and we kept watching it, we couldn't figure out what it was, not ever dreaming that we were going to run... dead into it. But all of a sudden, when we got out on this country road, it just set down, almost level with the treetops. Well, it had lit up the entire sky. Well it was seen as far as fifty miles away from where we were. But, on that country road, the lights were so bright, and the heat was so intense, I got out of the car. I don't know what my purpose was unless it was just normal instinct to think well, maybe I'd be safer outside than I would be inside. But tell you the truth, we thought the end of the world was coming. I mean we'd... I'd never in my life gone through such a situation. But I knew that there was no way we could go under it the way the fire was shooting out the bottom of it." You can read the entire interview at the *Computer UFO Network* (cufon.org).

Cabins in the Woods

When I first met Mike, he showed me an interesting picture of a beam of light captured at a cabin on a mountain in New Hampshire. During our interview we discussed the goings-on in that area, and it turns out, there is more going on in that area than at just that one cabin. He said, "There's two cabins, one on Black Mountain and the other is on Double Head Mountain; both in Jackson, New Hampshire." Black Mountain is typically known to many as an alpine ski area; Mike and some friends know it in a different way. He continued, "We had been doing 'contact circles' where I had a soundtrack of star sounds and we were meditating as a group once a week. There would be an intent on reaching out through non-physical means; attempting to get in contact with benevolent extraterrestrials. We had been doing this for a couple months and had been getting some strange things. We'd meditate and then compare notes and we got some common themes, similar sensations like hands going numb or heating up, and similar imagery like shapes, things like that. But one of the weirdest things that happened was that we all had missing time over at KRI. The minimum that we all agree on is fifteen minutes but may have been as long as a half hour. We didn't know this would happen, obviously, so we didn't keep an eye on the clock. We knew what time we started, we knew how long the soundtrack was and there was a solid fifteen minutes that no one can account for. At first no one noticed it, I was in a daze just staring at the clock and Val, one of the members of the group, said, 'You notice it, too.' Her saying that kinda snapped me out of it and we all started talking and did some math and found it was at least fifteen minutes." After that experience and with their training for the past couple of months, they wanted to take their contact circles out into the field. Mike said, "I had found these cabins that you could rent and there was very low light pollution, great view of the sky, and we thought it would be a good spot. We all hiked up and got settled, as it got dark, we all went outside and started our meditation. After that, we sat around looking at the sky and talked. It started getting late, around midnight, we're all tired and nothing was happening. We were about to give up when Val noticed it first. She said, 'Has that star been there the whole time?' We all look and were like, 'No…', as soon as we all acknowledged it, that's when it began moving and flashing. When it started moving, it was kinda like a falling leaf, swaying to the left and right as it descended from the sky. So, we decided to try and communicate with it somehow. We asked in our heads for it to make a perfect circle. It wasn't a circle, but it did make a teardrop shape and we were pretty impressed with that. We watched this thing for like forty-five minutes while asking it to do a bunch of things, like flash it's lights, things like that. Over the course of the night, we saw planes go by, and when they flew by, this thing would stop moving and dim its light. Once the planes would pass out of view, this thing would light up and start moving again."

    Mike told me that three of the people there that night were paranormal investigators, including himself, and not one of them thought to take a picture or video. They were caught up in the moment and I completely understood; it happened to me during one of my investigations. I was at a defunct Air Force base investigating lights that had been observed hovering around the area. I saw one and stared at it like an idiot with camera gear sitting right next to me. I shared that with Mike because I wanted him to know that even with our best intentions, we are human. He agreed and continued with his story, "It was starting to get less active, we're tired and were about to head in, and then Val saw a little red light drop out of the other light. The rest of us had a tree blocking our view of the light at that time, but what we saw was the whole sky flash red. That was kinda like our finale and that's when we turned in for the evening."

"Any other encounters at Black Mountain?" I asked. He said, "The other stuff happened at Double Head. I had gone up by myself on this one occasion and it was probably 8:30 or closer to 9pm. It had just gotten dark and I was sitting in the cabin. There's the center room with like a wood stove, benches, tables and four little bedrooms off to the side of it. I'm sitting in that main room and I see a white, flashing light outside, like someone was walking with a flashlight or something. I was like, well shit, I should probably go out and make sure they're not lost or that I might even have a guest for the night because they're not going to make it down the mountain at night. I got up and opened the door and as soon as I did that, I forgot why I was doing that because there's this brilliant, white light in the sky and it's just kinda strobing. It's at a distance, but it's intensely bright. I watch it for a few minutes, and I did manage to get a few pictures of it, but I took them with an old cell phone and it just looks like a dot in the sky. I don't remember anything else." I asked Mike if the light in the woods was reminiscent of the lights he saw as a child. He said, "Yeah, it was, but it's what drew my attention to go outside and felt like it wanted me to see the light in the sky or something."

I said, "Ok, well, tell me about that crazy light beam picture. How did all that happen?" I had only heard a brief version of the story a couple of years prior and I was hoping to get the longform version of it during our conversation.

He shared with me, "There was four of us up there, but two of them couldn't stay the next night, so it was just two of us. It was April, a nice sunny day and we're enjoying the weather then all of a sudden, we both got really tired. Like we were getting shut off like a light switch or something. We knew something was off, so we go in the cabin and try to keep each other up to see what would happen and we weren't ready for bed anyways. I decide to go out for a cigarette and that's what triggered the trail-cam to take a picture. I have no idea the picture is even there until I get home and get everything up on the laptop. But anyways, what I saw at the time, by the corner of the cabin, was like this six-foot-tall, maybe three-foot-wide shape. I call it an 'amoeba' but it was this light tan blob and it was huge. It comes out from the side of the cabin and just makes its way across my vision and into the woods and disappears. I'm like, 'Well, I don't know what the hell that was!' I snuff out my cigarette and go in. It was only after that I realized that it timed up with the light beam showing up." I asked Mike if the person inside the cabin noticed anything unusual during that time; they did not.

"Oh, the other thing that happened at Double Head," Mike interjected, "There was still snow up there in April, this was actually the night before the beam of light picture. There's four of us hiking, and with a 90-pound pack on, you'd go up to your knees in the snow in some spots." I let out a snicker. He continued, "These cabins were built in the 1920's but they updated the roofs to all tin; the snow would just slide right off of it and make these huge mounds in front of the door and all around it. So, to get into the cabin you'd have to climb over the snowbank and then step down and duck to open the front door and walk in. We're out there one night, about to walk in, and as I'm hunched over, I look into the woods and through the trees I see this huge, red ball of light. Everybody comes over to look and we're all just like, 'What the hell is that?' We decided to go around the back, there's a trail to a cliff with a nice view during the day and we're trying to creep out to the cliff to get a better look. When we got out there, we don't see the light, but the moon's there. But it's not the right color, it's too high in the sky, it's not the right size, and the light we saw was in the middle of the woods. It was strange." There were no other encounters for the rest of the night.

How It All Ends
(2016-Present)

*T*he culmination of anything can be described simply as an end point, the last stage of working toward something. In Mike's case, it would be reasonable to say that his lifelong culmination of encounters has been building toward… something, albeit unknown. The thing about the culmination of one's life is that it's not solely a conclusion. It's also about turning points, peaks and valleys, capstones, defeat, and growth. In a 1964 *Reader's Digest* article written by Charles Lindbergh, he said, "Life is a culmination of the past, an awareness of the present, an indication of a future beyond knowledge, the quality that gives a touch of divinity to matter."

In January of 2020, Mike entered his fourth

decade on Earth and by that time, his life had touched thousands of people; some in discord, most in synergy and I'm sure there are millions of us who could be described like that. Failure, dissonance, and incongruity happens, and that's ok, as long as it's accompanied by growth. Though his valleys can get low, his peaks are high. However, we can't always see it within ourselves and because of that, our actions and reactions can escalate to self-harm.

Trigger warning – some of the content contained in the following pages will discuss miscarriage, death, and suicide. People who have experienced traumatic experiences may be exposed to something that might trigger a physical and/or mental reaction.

If you need support at any time, please call the *National Suicide Prevention Hotline* at 1-800-273-8255.

Star Child
The subject of hybrid children within the realms of ufology is often controversial. Most serious researchers of the extraterrestrial phenomena see this area of their field bordering on absurdity brought on by attention seekers and is often not taken seriously. To get us all on the same page, the *Hybrid Children Community* website describes hybrid children as "…a genetic blend of human and extraterrestrial DNA." And that most believers of this phenomena think "…the children reside in a different dimension, but they will begin arriving on Earth in the relatively near future." Interestingly, a potential origin of this phenomena appears in Genesis: 6 1-4 which speaks of

the "Nephilim" who were "the offspring of the 'sons of God' and the 'daughters of men'." Genesis: 6 1-4 says in part, "...the Nephilim were on the earth in those days—and also afterward—when the sons of God went in unto the daughters of humans, who bore children to them."

Ufologists who study this phenomenon have found that a large percentage of reports come from female abductees. Women have described these encounters as starting with an abduction by extraterrestrials, being placed on examination tables, and then an unearthly version of in vitro fertilization takes place. It is reported that this procedure aids in incubation but then the fetus is removed at an early stage, during another abduction, and placed into artificial wombs. The women are then taken again and are allowed to spend time with their hybrid children. This is reportedly to "...instill an emotional bond between the abductee and the hybrid," the purpose of which is unknown. It has also been reported that at some point during this process, in the abductee's earthly life, they may have felt or known that they were pregnant and tragically miscarried. In some cases, woman have visited their doctors where evidence of endometrial scratching has been observed. This type of scratching is a known medical procedure and is performed to aid an embryo's implant into the uterus preceding in vitro fertilization; the procedure itself is considered by some to be controversial in its own right. Some cases of the hybrid procedure involve men. While the abduction is not nearly as invasive, some of the trauma inducing aftermath can be.

In my discussion with Mike, he opened up about some peculiar incidents; one took place at the KRI Center. He was there early one morning to get a jump on preparing the center for an Equinox event they were hosting later that night. He shared with me, "I was setting up for the event and it was like four in the morning. I was grabbing beanbag chairs and bringing them downstairs, bringing cables upstairs, just setting up, ya know? After a bit, I went up the back stairwell to go outside to have a cigarette. I look up, there's this one star twinkling just a little. I'm tired and acting a little goofy and I say, 'Ah, there's always that one star that twinkles just a little too brightly.' I was just saying it to myself, ya know? And as soon as I said that, this star started moving and making a perfect circle in the sky. It freaked me out, so I threw my cigarette out and friggin' ran back in and down the stairs. I then needed to go up the front stairs to the front part of KRI to the main lobby. While I was in that front stairwell, I hear this little girl laugh. So, now I'm in a complete fucking panic. I'm like, 'Alright, they're outside, this place is haunted, and I've got nowhere to run. What the fuck is going on?'" In Mike's frightened state, all he could think of to do was to sit in Andy's office and try to calm himself down. He eventually sought out Andy who lived in an apartment at the Center. Mike said, "Andy's apartment is right behind his office, so after a while, I breakdown and I pound on Andy's door. He finally gets up and he's like, 'What the fuck man? It's early.' I told him what was happening, and I just needed someone to talk to." The situation, and Mike, eventually settled down.

The following year, in 2017, Mike had taken a weekend camping trip to Pittsburgh, New Hampshire. He spent a few days watching for moose, enjoying the lake, and having some time to himself. On his third and final day of camping, a curious event occurred. The day started normal enough, he made coffee and food but later on, he mysteriously woke up on the ground. He does not remember falling, nothing seemed to hurt, he was just lying on the ground seemingly placed there. Mike thought about the event throughout the day and just couldn't shake the feeling that something more happened than he remembered, an occurrence he's grown accustomed to. While camping, Mike isn't one to keep close track of time, but he knew a lot of it had passed when he woke up on the ground. His last memory was of the morning, and when he woke up, it was afternoon. He cannot say for sure, but he felt some missing time occurred.

As time went on and Mike grew further removed from both the KRI Center and camping incidents, he almost forgot about them completely until another event occurred in January of 2019. He revealed, "I'm still with my ex-girlfriend at this point, we're having a normal night. I mean, we're not talking about any weird shit, considering what we both do. We eat dinner and we're watching that *Ray* movie; we're not even watching a creepy movie or anything. Anyways, I eat about three times the speed of light compared to her, ya know?" I have another snicker, one of what seemed like a thousand throughout our conversation. He continued, "I finished eating and said I was going out to have a cigarette. So, I go out on the porch, I'm having a cigarette and I'm not thinking about UFOs, no business shit that's coming up that's on my mind, I'm just trying to have five minutes of peace. Like, for once in my life, I'm just a normal fucking person for five minutes." We laugh uproariously at this comment but the solemnity of it was not lost on us. He's exasperated and always exhausted; he doesn't sleep enough and lives off coffee and cigarettes. A lot of us have been there, but not for his reasons. Even though he's accepted what's happening to him, I can't imagine that makes it easier to get through. Back to Mike: "I look up at the sky, I don't see anything twinkle, nothing to draw my attention, just normal. Then all of a sudden, this fucking feeling just comes in out of nowhere and fucking hits me. It's a message, is what it is. And it's, 'You have a daughter out here and you'll see her within the next year.'" In case that's not clear, what Mike is saying here is that he has just been cosmically/telepathically sent a message from extraterrestrials and told that he has an alien/human hybrid daughter. I know, it's wild. Mike thinks so, too. I had known about this incident before both of my interviews with him. He is quite open about his experiences and shared a brief version of the message on his social media. Many of the comments were of a supporting nature and when I read it, I wasn't sure what to think. I'm sure I had another moment of, "I just need to process that for a second." He and I briefly discussed it around the time he shared it online and we both didn't know what to make of it. He continued, "It hit me out of the fucking blue and crippled me, really. So, I walk back into the house crying and she asked what was wrong. I told her what happened. Nothing's come of it, I'm about a month out from it being a year, so I don't know."

It was during this time that Mike remembered the incidents from camping and KRI. While processing the message of a hybrid daughter, he thought the two incidents might be related. There's a possible correlation to seeing the light that early morning at the center and hearing the child's laughter. Perhaps it was the extraterrestrial's way of easing him into the knowledge of an alien/human hybrid daughter; that ole "tinkering" coming back into play. Maybe the KRI incident was a message that was too vague for Mike to understand. He said, "At the time, I didn't connect the laughter to the sighting." And perhaps the missing time that he experienced while camping was one of those "bonding" moments described by other abductees with hybrid children. And lastly, since Mike wasn't getting the hint from the other two incidents, the extraterrestrials decided to send Mike a stronger, more concise message. If so, he got it loud and clear.

Mike fully understands and admits that all of the information presented about a possible hybrid child is anecdotal and speculation at best. He did want it included in this book because it is a part of his total experience. It is his perception and perspective of the events as they unfolded before him and he would like everything represented equally. It is my privilege and pleasure to do that for him. Mike probably summed it up best when he said, "Shit happens, can you prove it? Absolutely not. We ain't proved shit yet, we're still fighting about it. Let people tell their stories." As of this writing, nothing further has come from Mike's message.

Moonrise Kingdom

Mike looks forward to the summer months and tries to campout as much as possible. During one trip a couple of years ago, he and an ex-girlfriend sighted a UFO while driving into their campsite. They had set up their site earlier in the day, had a meeting at KRI, and then drove back that night to campout for the weekend. As they pulled into the parking area, they both saw a light in the sky. Mike said, "It's bigger than a star, bigger than a planet, but not as big as the moon. We're watching it as we pull in, we park, and it's not moving. We still had to get to the campsite, so we're like, 'Whatever…' and walk down to the site. We go to bed; nothing happens, and we wake up in the morning and get coffee going. There's shitty reception out there, so I can't check my messages, but I have another meeting at KRI later and that's when all my messages come in. There was a woman from the previous meeting who had sent me a message about seeing a strange light in the sky at the same time that we had. So, I was like, well, if it was the same light, that's weird but I didn't think too much about it. We finish that meeting, drive back to the campsite and we're walking the trail to our camp. I'm used to the woods at night, nothing really bothers me but I'm feeling really anxious. I ask my ex-girlfriend if she's feeling anxious too and she says, 'My anxiety is going wicked hard right now, what's going on?' We both acknowledged that something was off, our anxiety is high, so we just try to make a normal night of things. I get a fire going so we can eat and then that's when we noticed a light in the sky. It's kinda diving in and out of the trees, getting lower. She said that she was getting impressions that there were beings on the ground and giving her a scenario of working on a car kinda thing. Like, she knew that wasn't really what was happening, but that's what they were trying to sell." I chuckle again. "Eventually we're both like, 'Whatever this is, if they're coming, they're coming, nothing we can do,' so we just decide to go to bed. After a little while, we saw this glowing light out in the woods. We both acknowledged it, but then thought it was best to just go back to sleep. When we woke up, she noticed that she had this huge bruise on her inner thigh. It hadn't been there the day before and we noticed puncture marks within the bruise. I had the same mark on my leg the week earlier but assumed I had just knocked my leg on something. I'm always rough and tumble with things and am always hitting into something." For a few days after that incident, Mike said they both saw lights in the sky near their homes. Typically seen outside their bedroom windows. They told some mutual experiencers about the incident who said that they too had experienced similar bruising. The implication here is that a possible abduction occurred, and Mike felt terrible that he potentially brought another person into his extraterrestrial experiences.

One person that Mike never wanted involved with the aliens was his daughter. Regrettably, that may have happened one night when he took her and one of her friends camping. The girls experienced missing time and were inexplicably brought to a different area of the campsite while having no memory of what occurred. Mike explained, "I took her and a friend out camping and later on in the night, my daughter had to go pee. I told her to just go in the woods, but she wanted to walk back up to the parking lot with her friend so they could use their phones one more time, reception was better up there, and there was a bathroom. Her friend fell asleep earlier and while we were talking about them going up to the parking lot, this loud humming noise just started out of the blue. There was no boat on the water, we thought maybe a drone flying around, you're just looking for some type of excuse. The longer it goes on, the louder it got, and it kinda enveloped the whole place, the whole site. It was loud enough to wake up her friend who came out of the tent and was like, 'What the hell is going on?' So, eventually it just kinda stopped. We thought it was weird, but they ended up going to the bathroom. They seemed to be gone for a while, but I'm not worried about it, figured they were just playing on their phones. Finally, I hear this crashing through the woods, and I'm like, 'What the fuck?' It's the two girls and they're exasperated. I asked them what was going on and they're like, 'We went to the bathroom, checked our phones and we were walking back down the trail to the campsite.' I'm like, 'Ok…' and I'm not thinking anything about UFOs, but I was like, 'Wait, why are you two coming in from over there?' She said, 'We're like ten, fifteen feet into the trail and we hear an owl. The next thing I know, we climbed up this hill and we're at the bathrooms on the opposite side of the campgrounds.' They're both working through this, trying to figure it out, retelling the story. She was like, 'You know how long that would have taken? Like, there's no way we could have gotten from here to here, step off the trail and manage to walk through the woods to the other side.' She said once they realized where they were, they walked from those other bathrooms, down the main road and back over to here. They got on the trail again to our campsite and then lost the trail. They're totally confused on why they can't see the trail. It was so strange. The funny and ironic part is that I had this alien head lantern thing, and they saw that light to lead them back to the site."

It Flew Right Over the Car
In 1959, a B52C Stratofortress Bomber crashed into Spruce Swamp, located in Fremont, New Hampshire. The Union Leader newspaper wrote, "The plane's eight-man crew all survived by bailing out shortly before the Cold War-era bomber dropped out of the New Hampshire sky Aug. 10, 1959." A few months after the camping trip with his daughter, Mike went out to Spruce Swamp with Dean and Pam Merchant along with some other friends. He told me, "We had spent the day in Freemont at Spruce Swamp. My buddy knew where the wreckage was, and we decided to make a day of it." Merchant has conducted extensive research into the crash along with a possible connection to an unknown intelligence. The plane's original purpose was to conduct training exercises in the southeast U.S. but due to some mechanical issues and foul weather, was redirected to Goose Base in Labrador, Canada. Coincidentally, the area was riddled with UFO activity at the time of the crash.

There are some interesting reports from 1948-1953 wherein radar picked up numerous unidentified aerial phenomena activity during that time frame.

Personnel at the Goose Bay Base were unable to identify their targets. One such case was reported to NICAP by Major Edwin A. Jerome, USAF (Ret.). It read in part, "While inspecting the USAF radar shack, the operator noted a high-speed target on his scope going from NE to SW. Upon computation of the speed it was found to be about 9000 mph. This incident caused much consternation in the shack since obviously this was no time for levity or miscalculations in the presence of an inspecting party." "…the target appeared and this time the inspectors were actually shown the apparition on the radar screen. The only reaction to this was that obviously the American equipment was way off calibration." "The prevailing theory at the time was that it was a meteor. I personally discounted this since upon interviewing the radar observers on both sides of the base they stated that it maintained an altitude of 60,000 feet and a speed of approximately 9000 mph. To make this story more incredible, the very next day both radars again reported an object hovering over the base at about 10 mph, at 45,000 feet. The 'official' story on this was that they were probably some type of 'high-flying sea gulls.' You must remember all these incidents happened before the days of fast, high flying jets and missiles and the now common altitude record-breaking helicopters."

Incredibly, I found another report of a UFO from the same year *and* month of the B52C crash. It stated in part, "August 1959 USAF SAC Base, Goose Bay, Labrador. At the time I was 22 years old and a Newfoundlander working in the Motor Pool on the Base. The event happened at approximately 0300 hours. I had been called out to drive two (2) visiting

USAF pilots to a lake near the Pine Tree Radar Base (approximately 25 - 30 miles from the Air Base) to do some fishing before they returned to their home base." "We were driving along when the passenger in the right-hand seat said 'what the hell is that'. I looked out my window and saw something coming over the trees and I immediately stopped the jeep in the middle of the road and all three of us got out. What we saw was unbelievable." "It was flying parallel to the ground and going very slow. It made a slight humming sound, but it did not make any other noise. There were no flashing lights whatsoever. What it did have was three large round lit areas running in a straight line." "The color was a yellow/white, but leaning more to the white. I can state all this with great clarity because there was only about 150 feet between the craft and the ground. It moved very slowly and took a good 45 - 60 seconds to cross the width of the road. After it reached the opposite side of the road it disappeared from sight, because of the tall trees." "The Control Tower was notified by my two-way radio. The people in the tower saw the object, however no one did anything about it...."

Mike continued, "So, that was kind of our angle for going out there to take a look at everything." He has a piece of that plane hanging in his office, and a picture of it is in this book. He further stated, "After the swamp, we went to the house of one of the experiencers that I work with. I sat with them and their family for a while, and then I left with another friend to go home for the night. On our drive, I saw this light. I said, 'Hey, there's something in the sky right there.' My friend was tired and said, 'I'm so tired right now, I don't care, just tell me when and if I need to pull over.' So, I'm watching this thing track across the sky and I'm thinking, 'That ain't right, that ain't right, that ain't right.' Because we were driving, I lose it between the trees. I see it again finally, on the other side of the road, right by the public works building in South Berwick, Maine. I told her, 'You need to stop now and back up ten feet.' She does and this fucking huge craft comes right over us. We turn the radio off put the windows down. We both saw it come right over us." The craft flew off quickly, and the pair were only left with the memory of the encounter. In their discussion and comparisons of what they saw, they found that their descriptions didn't match. Mike said, "Neither of us had any missing time or anything, but she remembers seeing it from the bottom and I remember seeing it from the top. There's no reason I should have seen it from the top. She was like, 'Well how the fuck did you see the top of it?' I was like, 'I don't know!'" Mike is just so confused by it all, he ruminated, "Where do you break this shit down? Is it extraterrestrial, is it spiritual, is it consciousness? I don't know. I assume there's a bigger picture out there than anyone has been led to believe. Do I have the answers to that? Hell fucking no. But, is this something we should examine or include in the discussion? Absolutely."

Concerning the Mind

In this section, I am going to start with addressing some aspects of my own mental health. The reason I want to do this is twofold; I want to do this because of what Mike is about to share *and* I would like this writing to be another example of normalizing discussions surrounding mental health. By doing so, we can create a safe and caring environment for the people we love to reach out to us anytime, especially in a time of need.

    I have experienced loss, heartbreak, low self-worth, a longing to be loved, and a million other things that everyone else has experienced. I'm not unique in that regard. One aspect of our individuality that does make us unique is how we respond when faced with negativity. For me, my responses throughout childhood, adolescence, and early adulthood would be considered less than healthy. Some of that includes overeating, negative self-talk, toxic relationships, drug use, alcohol use, inaction, lack of growth, and more. Throughout the years, I have developed healthier coping mechanisms when faced with difficulties in my life. Some of that has come from a therapist, some from friends and family, some from books, and many other sources, but no matter where it comes from, it always ends with me and the choices I make. As I've established, I don't always make the best ones, but I am trying. It doesn't always work out and I'm not always fair with myself and sometimes with others, but I am trying. Total happiness still eludes me, but I am trying. Anxiety and depression are a part of my life, trauma is a part of my life, occasional suicidal thoughts are a part of my life. That might seem messy or dark, but I disagree, it's normal.

    In speaking with a friend during the writing of this book we organically came up with a phrase through conversation that helped me. In my opinion, it's the most concise and filled-with-hope sentence that I have ever uttered. It is, "Broken, but trying." I know that it's not profound; it's simple, but it works for me. What I feel when I speak or read that sentence is an acknowledgement of my past, keeping an eye on my present, and setting goals for my future. It's powerful to me. It helps me, though not every time, and that's ok. All of this is ok. It's us, it's human, and as long as I choose life, I get to keep trying. Same goes for you.

Mike has had concerns with his own mental health. I have seen him make some of those unhealthy choices. Though I am not with him often, I have also witnessed some of his healthier choices. During our conversation, he shared with me something that changed his life and will hopefully lead to even more healthy choices. Before we get to that, I would like to share what life has been like for Mike in 2019. He said to me, "Around June is when I quit my job. I wasn't in a good headspace, and the kind of work I did, you go on the job site and there's jabbing and jarring all day. Supposed to be only jokes, but it got to me." Mike was a laborer for a commercial flooring company. He was working so much that he barely had time to sleep, let alone help others in the experiencer community. It was all taking a toll on him. He also found out that some of his co-workers had accessed his Facebook page and were unkind about the extraterrestrial nature of his interests. It all reached an apex and he resigned. He had a bit of a nest egg and figured he'd be fine for a while but as the summer wore on, his financial situation worsened. He knew he had to find work, but he had also made commitments to experiencers in the community, the Exeter UFO Festival, and the Greater New England UFO Conference in Leominster, Massachusetts. Despite the commitments and financial woes, he felt that he could find work after everything had finished up. He said, "I couldn't get a job and then ask for this weekend off and then that weekend off, ya know? I knew I'd find something later." As the Exeter festival neared, he pushed his problems to the side and became excited to see old friends, host the trolley rides, and to just be generally ensconced into the UFO community; that's where he felt most comfortable.

After the Exeter festival, his depression returned. He felt useless, he endlessly missed his UFO friends and found that he was without hope. It was at this time that Mike made the decision to end his life. He told me, "I was just done, with everything. I'm 40 years old, no job, and the only thing I got going for me is the UFO stuff. Even that wasn't enough. I was just stuck in my head and couldn't get over the fact that my life sucked, and I didn't want to keep living with it like that." As I listened to him describe his suicide plan, an exceptional sorrow washed over me. "I had it all planned out," he shared. "I was going to get some sleeping pills and my Elysian Space Dust beer, that's my favorite. I was going to drive out to an old camping spot I knew. I'd build a fire, drink some beers, and take the pills so they'd interact with the alcohol. I figured I'd drink for a while and then hang myself."

My eyes watered when he told me that. "Jesus, Mike," I said. "When did everything change?"

Mike was getting ready to go to sleep on Sunday September 8, 2019 while making his plan. He shared, "I'm just lying in bed, mind-mapping all this stuff out in the complete darkness, ya know? Obviously, I had given up. And, for whatever reason, I don't know, I got bored or whatever, I picked up my phone, and started scrolling through Facebook. That's when I saw the message from Michelle Mitchell." Michael Mitchell, Michelle's husband, unexpectedly passed away that day. It came as a complete shock to everyone and numerous posts filled his Facebook wall with condolences, stories, and pictures of his art. Mike and Michael had been friends for a few years and met because of their mutual interest in the UFO subject. Michael was a comic book artist and publisher and had released a lot of independent comic books, one in particular had covered the Exeter Incident and was a local favorite amongst enthusiasts. Mike said of seeing the post, "My first reaction was that this was somebody's idea of a sick joke. I just saw him a week ago at the festival, there's no way… I couldn't believe it. I was in shock. I thought the next day, this will all get cleared up, the account got hacked or something. The further it went along, I was like, 'Holy shit, this is real.' Just the impact it had on me was tremendous."

    I met Michael and his wife briefly at a conference in 2018 and I was quite impressed with his work. Anybody who had met the couple couldn't say enough good things about them; his passing truly had a tragic impact in his wide circle of family, friends, and fans. Mike continued, "He was such a great guy, he loved life. Always just top-notch guy, first one there to help you if you needed anything. Over the years we developed a pretty good relationship and just the way it hit me and reading all the comments, how it hit everybody else…" At this point, Mike was at a loss for words. He paused, gathered his thoughts, and said, "Before, I felt bad about myself. When this hit me, it… it was different. I was sad. I was crushed. I don't know how to define it by words but there's a difference." Mike was describing true grief. He continued, "Finally something clicked, and I thought, 'This is what you're going to do to other people if you go through with it. You can't do that to people.' I had a moment where I had to grab myself by the bootstraps and say, 'Tomorrow is not in stone, you can get through it. Your life is shitty, but you can get through it.'" After he said that, I shared with Mike that I had a similar thought process a few years prior and it had worked for me, too. I couldn't put someone through that grief. Mike said, "Yeah, it's a powerful thing apparently." We laughed at that together and then I asked him if he had shared with Michelle that Michael's death had saved his life. He said, "Yeah, actually, I told her in October. Besides you, she's the only other person I've told. Then we went to the funeral. That played into my decision, too. Being there was hard, I just couldn't deliberately do that to the people that love me." I wiped away tears while Mike described the funeral. Those words are not for this book, but I was thankful to have heard them. I then went back to read all the comments and stories from Michael's Facebook page. Such a loss. Rest in peace Michael.

    I asked Mike if he had reached out to anybody

for help during this time. "No," he said. "I'd just isolate myself, and if there was a meeting or something, I'd show up, be polite, but not say too much." After the funeral, Mike explained, he realized that he meant something to people. He said, "I'm not just this isolated, miserable piece of shit, ya know? There would be an effect on people if I just disappeared."

I then asked him, "Ok, where was your headspace after all of that. You're trying now, you're surviving. What's changed?"

He shared, "Well, then another big change happened. My headspace is better, life not so much but I'm getting through it. I'm making a plan to dig myself out of this hole and then November hits and we decide to close down the Center." During this timeframe, Mike was living at KRI and their funding was tight with the majority of it coming out of the pocket of Andy Kitt. With the Center closing, all that Mike held dear was slipping away. Not only was he losing a place to live, he was losing a place for their collective groups to convene. Mike, Andy, and Val had spent years building a community and the emotional aspect to the Center closing was felt by many. "That was the next big hurdle to get through," he said. "It was a triple headed beast for me. It was all of a sudden, a major time limit thing to get everything moved. There was no time to be emotional, but it would hit me from time to time. We had a month to do it with a holiday in the middle of it. And, the third part of it for me was… I was living there as well."

Mike's work with the experiencer community is so important to him, that a few days after their decision to close the Center, he went looking for a new space to hold meetings; not a place to live. In my opinion, his dedication is unreal. He shared, "Alright, it's so important to me, I had to find a space. A woman who worked at KRI years back, I walked down to her space and thought I might be able to use a small portion of her space when she wasn't using it so I could have small meetings. When I talked to her, she just threw me the keys and said, 'Yeah, the whole back of the office hasn't been used since the other person left, it's just sitting here empty. Yeah, make it yours.' That was a huge stress reliever to have a landing place for the groups. I put so much work into the group and for that not to crumble was hugely beneficial for the group and my mental wellbeing. Knowing that was secure gave me more reason to keep fighting."

Mike's other hurdle was a living space. As of this writing, Mike is homeless, but as he tells it, it's working for him. He told me, "I love camping, anybody who knows me knows that. I have all this gear and stuff and a minivan. The backseat isn't quite big enough for a six-foot man to stretch out on, but if the window is down, I can make it work. I decide I'm going to do this car-camping thing. Everybody who knew I was going to do this was kinda worried. When I was going through everything we just talked about, I was in a place where I got complacent and allowed myself to get into that headspace. Now, with this living arrangement, there's some challenges that come along with it, some stuff is not easy, but that's kinda the part I'm ok with. I remember being in that headspace where I didn't want to live, now I'm in a situation where if I'm not proactive in thinking ahead, and planning things out to stay alive, I won't. It's weird when you're in that depressed state and you want to die, or think you do, but when you're forced into the physical challenge of survival, you react to it, you respond to it. Even though it's a challenge, it's that total mindset that I enjoy." While some might think that is odd, I can see the logic in it and it truly seems like a healthy way to look at the situation. He did share with me that he does not want to live like that forever, or even that much longer, and is actively trying to get himself to a better situation. He said his biggest challenge right now is that everyone that cares for him is worried about him. He said, "I'm ok! They know I'm stubborn, that's what they're worried about. Will I tell them when I really need help? That's the question, ya know?" He will. I'm sure of this because Mike has decided to choose life.

Epilogue

Mike's nightmarish encounters grew to a point of acceptance over time as an adult, but during childhood, he rarely spoke about his experiences. He shared with me, "I grew up in a family where we didn't talk about UFOs; ghosts were fine, that's acceptable. I don't think UFOs were unacceptable, it's just that it never came up. It was never discussed. I get the marker put up and that goes out to the news and it kinda travels through the family. And that's when the stories started coming out." His parents told him about a sighting they had before he was born. He said, "There was an object in the sky, and they pulled over to watch it. They weren't the only ones; others had pulled over to watch it, as well. Everybody just kinda watched this thing float in the sky in Hampton."

Mike's daughter had another brush with the

extraterrestrials one night while with a group of friends; they all saw the same thing. Mike said, "They had all walked down to a Cumberland Farms that wasn't far from the house. While they were in the store, somebody came in and said that there was a UFO outside. They all thought, 'Bullshit,' and went outside to look. They get out there and they see this giant, orange sphere above Main St. One of them said that it was the moon but then it started moving down the street. They ran as fast as they could to another friend's house."

Mike was also told a story about how his great uncle had been kicked out of Brewster Academy, a boarding school in Wolfeboro, New Hampshire, because he told everyone that he had been abducted by aliens. Mike explained, "The school said it was a mental illness or drugs and were unequipped to handle it. His sister remembered that he had to go see a special doctor in Boston about it but was not privy to what the meeting with the doctor was about. Also, my grandfather, if you remember the *Intruders* story, it turns out he had quite the collection of books and articles on the crash at Roswell. He rolled his eyes at me because of that book choice when he's got his own little secret. It almost seemed that he was trying to give hints about his interest. He ran an autobody business and he named it "Sky Wind", and he was a big, Italian dude, looked like he was in the Mafia, there's stories that he might have been…," we laughed, "…but not the type of guy you would think would have a favorite flower, but he did. Stargazer Lilies. Also, his house was historically considered haunted, by all of us." Mike further explained that his grandfather had predicted the day that Mike would be born, which was an entire month after the due date. "They wouldn't let you go that long now," Mike explained, "but he was right."

Mike and I both questioned the rolling of his grandfather's eyes when Mike had picked out the *Intruders* book. We surmised that his grandfather might have thought, "Oh great, this kid is involved with them, too." We shared a chuckle over that, but perhaps it was true. When I asked Mike if his grandfather had any extraterrestrial encounters of his own, he said there were none that he knew about but added, "Aside from it just affecting me, it's trickled down to everyone else it seems. Everyone has had their own little touch with it."

In my opinion, the greatest part about Mike's story is that it's not over. He could have followed through with his plan and maybe I would be writing this at the request of a loved one, or worse, his story may have never been told. While the extraterrestrial background of his life is what brought this project to fruition, it's not the whole story. We found a person. Broken, but trying. Traumatized, but surviving. And I say "we" because you and I found him together. He was hidden beneath a cacophony of lights in the sky, creatures in a bedroom, a daughter, a failed marriage, suicidal thoughts, friendship, hope, and the will to live. At the time of this writing, I had no idea that this is where we would be: To find a man once lost within his trauma able to emerge on the other side, scarred but ready to keep going.

The totality of his story unfolded before me as it did for you. I laughed and cried with him. I was scared when he was and found humor in the small moments. He stood proudly in the back of the KRI Center during the presentations I had given there, as I'm sure he did for others, but right now, in this moment, he is the one that I am proud of. More encounters will happen, more stories will be told, more trauma will create more scars, but he's different now. Not in personality but in mindset. He wants to live, and he knows what comes with that. The challenges of the extraterrestrial encounters, the challenges of being homeless, the challenges of a father, friend, and supporter come with that and he's better because of it. He's stronger than ever.

There's a quote from the blog *The Secret Circle* that's speaks to the survival of trauma a hell of a lot better than I ever could. It states, "You do not have to suffer any more. You do not have to be victimized by experiences you never asked for. It is not your fault! You have the smallest bit of hope still in your heart, otherwise you wouldn't be here. Use that hope, magnify it and mold it. Recreate yourself, rebuild. You deserve it, you are worthy of it. You can be healed! For every ounce of weight you are trapped beneath now, you can transform into strength. There is still a place for you on this Earth. There is still a life to be experienced that is more beautiful than I could possibly describe, and it's all yours. There is light and there is love for you."

Bibliography

"60 Years Later: Fremont B-52 Crash In 1959 Receives Renewed Scrutiny". *Union Leader*, 2019, https://www.unionleader.com/news/veterans/years-later-fremont-b--crash-in-receives-renewed-scrutiny/article_08130525-d016-5e96-a697-3c333e117ad0.html.

"Asogian/Legends". *Wookieepedia*, https://starwars.fandom.com/wiki/Asogian/Legends.

"Bergstrom AFB Interview of Betty Cash, Vickie & Colby Landrum, Part 1 of 2". *Cufon.org*, http://www.cufon.org/cufon/cashlani.htm.

"Blue Aliens with Blue Skin". *Hybridsrising.Com*, 2013-2019, http://hybridsrising.com/Hybrid-Project/Hybrids-Rising-The-Blues-HP.html.

"Blue Jay - Spirit Animal, Symbolism and Meaning". *Dreamingandsleeping.com*, https://dreamingandsleeping.com/blue-jay-spirit-animal-symbolism-and-meaning/.

"Dover Demon". *Cryptid Wiki*, http://cryptidz.wikia.com/wiki/Dover_Demon.

"Exeter UFO Festival". *Exeter UFO Festival*. http://www.exeterufofestival.org/ 2014.

"Genesis 6 / Hebrew - English Bible / Mechon-Mamre". *Mechon-Mamre.Org*, http://www.mechon-mamre.org/p/pt/pt0106.htm.

"Healing Crystals and Stones – Legends of America". *Legendsofamerica.com*, https://www.legendsofamerica.com/na-healingstones/.

"Historic Flood Spring 1987". *Weather.gov*, https://www.weather.gov/nerfc/hf_spring_1987.

"Moon Phases Calendar for September 1997 - Calendar-12.com". *Calendar-12.com*, 2011, https://www.calendar-12.com/moon_calendar/1997/september.

"NH State Parks". *WHITE LAKE STATE PARK*, 2017, https://www.nhstateparks.org/visit/state-parks/white-lake-state-park.

"NOVA Online/Kidnapped by UFOs". *Pbs.Org*, https://www.pbs.org/wgbh/nova/aliens/johnmack.html.

"Post-Trauma No More". *The Secret Circle*, 2019, https://thesecretcircle.home.blog/.

"Snowy Owl | Nongame | New Hampshire Fish and Game Department". *Wildlife.State.Nh.Us*, https://www.wildlife.state.nh.us/wildlife/profiles/snowy-owl.html.

"The Psychology of Triggers and How They Affect Mental Health". *Goodtherapy.Org Therapy Blog*, 2019, https://www.goodtherapy.org/blog/psychpedia/trigger

"The UFO Incident (TV Movie 1975) - Imdb". https://www.imdb.com/title/tt0073834/.

"UFO Investigator". *Nicap.org*, 1973, http://www.nicap.org/madar/articles/197303XXstudy_conducted_at_exeter.pdf.

"Y2K Bug". *National Geographic Society*, https://www.nationalgeographic.org/encyclopedia/Y2K-bug/.
Berry, Michael.

Berry, Michael. "New Hampshire's UFO History and The Exeter UFO Festival". *New Hampshire Magazine*. https://www.nhmagazine.com/ufos-in-new-hampshire/. 2015.

Brindley, Michael. "Marking History: The Betty and Barney Hill Incident in Lincoln". *Nhpr.org*, 2014, https://www.nhpr.org/post/marking-history-betty-and-barney-hill-incident-lincoln#stream/0.

Brock, Bill. "Rogue Mysteries | Prime Video". *Amazon*. https://www.amazon.com/Rogue-Mysteries/dp/B07LFLLZH7. 2018

Cajori, Florian. A History of Mathematical Notations. United States, Dover Publications, 2013.

Coleman, Loren. "1893 "Dover Demon"". *Cryptomundo.com*, 2009, http://cryptomundo.com/cryptozoo-news/dd-1893/.

Coleman, Loren. *Monsters Of Massachusetts*. Stackpole Books, 2013.

Coleman, Loren. "The Dover Demon's Men in Black". *Cryptozoonews.com*, 2016, http://www.cryptozoonews.com/dover-mibs/.

Coolidge, Frederick L. "Sigmund Freud and Alien Abduction Stories". *Psychology Today*, 2013, https://www.psychologytoday.com/us/blog/how-think-neandertal/201311/sigmund-freud-and-alien-abduction-stories.

Fontaine, R.A. "Flood of April 1987 In Maine, Massachusetts, And New Hampshire". *United States Geological Survey*, 1987, https://pubs.er.usgs.gov/publication/ofr87460.

Forest, Christopher. *Curious Creatures of New England*. Schiffer, 2013.

Fuller, John G. *Incident at Exeter*. New York: Putnam, 1974.

Fuller, John G. *The Interrupted Journey*. New York: Dial Press, 1966.

Gaia Staff. "RH Negative Blood - Abducted by Aliens | Gaia". *Gaia*, July 31, 2018, https://www.gaia.com/article/rh-negative-blood-abducted-aliens.

Galan, Nicole, and Carissa Stephens. "Blue Baby Syndrome: Causes, Symptoms, And Treatments". *Medical News Today*, May 29, 2018, https://www.medicalnewstoday.com/articles/321955.php#causes.

Granite Sky Services. (2019). *Granite Sky Services*. https://granitesky.org/services

Grant, Oliver. "Are Aliens Tracking Abductees with Implants?". *UFO Insight*, 2017, https://www.ufoinsight.com/aliens-tracking-abductees-implants/.

Hall, Richard. "Major Edwin A. Jerome, USAF (Ret.) Reports Ufos Over Goose Bay, Summer 1948". *Project1947.com*, http://www.project1947.com/folio/1948_labrador.htm

Hind, Angela. "BBC News | Alien Thinking". *News.Bbc.co.uk*, 2005 http://news.bbc.co.uk/2/hi/uk_news/magazine/4071124.stm.

Hufford, David J., Dr. *Wonders in the Sky: Unexplained Aerial Objects from Antiquity to Modern Times*. Foreword. Camberwell: Jeremy P. Tarcher/Penguin, 2009.

Jones, Bob. "Goose Bay UFO Incident". *C-And-E-Museum.org*, http://www.c-and emuseum.org/Pinetreeline/other/other19/other19j.html.

Keel, John A. *The Mothman Prophecies: A True Story*. United States, Tom Doherty Associates, 2002.

Kirchofer, Gregory. *2017 Water Quality Report*. Town of Somersworth, Somersworth, 2017, https://www.somersworth.com/sites/somersworthnh/files/uploads/2017_water_quality_report.pdf.

Lenzer, Jeanne. "John E Mack". *National Center for Biotechnology Information, U.S. National Library of Medicine*, 2004, https://www.ncbi.nlm.nih.gov/pmc/articles/PMC523131/.

Lowth, Marcus. "The Connection of Alien Contact and Sudden Psychic Ability". *UFO Insight*, 2018, https://www.ufoinsight.com/the-connection-of-alien-contact-and-sudden-psychic-ability/.

Marden, Kathleen, and Stanton T Friedman. *Captured! The Betty and Barney Hill UFO Experience: The True Story of the World's First Documented Alien Abduction*. New Page Books, 2007.

Marden, Kathleen. "Kathleenmardenufo". *Kathleen-Marden.Com*, 2019, https://www.kathleen-marden.com/.

Marden, Kathleen. "New Hampshire Commemorates Betty and Barney Hill UFO Experience". *Openminds.Tv*, 2011, http://www.openminds.tv/nh-commemorates-hill-ufo-experience-740/11115.

Merchant, Dean. "Close Encounters of the Second Kind in Stratham". *Seacoastonline.com*, 2008, https://www.seacoastonline.com/article/20080512/LIFE/80512030.

Miller, Chuck. "UFO FYI: Creature Files- The "Dover Demon"". *Ufofyi.Blogspot.com*, 2009, http://ufofyi.blogspot.com/2009/08/ufo-fyi-creature-files-dover-demon.html.

Morabito, L. A. et al. "Discovery of Currently Active Extraterrestrial Volcanism". *Science*, vol 204, no. 4396, 1979, pp. 972-972. *American Association for The Advancement Of Science (AAAS)*, doi:10.1126/science.204.4396.972.

Morphy, Rob. "DOVER DEMON: (MASSACHUSETTS, USA)". *Cryptopia.us*, 2010, http://www.cryptopia.us/site/2010/03/dover-demon-massachusetts-usa/.

Nielsen, Bridget. "Frequently Asked Questions | Hybrid Children Community". *Hybridchildrencommunity.com*, 2013, https://www.hybridchildrencommunity.com/frequently-asked-questions/.

New York Times. "SCIENTISTS SAY COMET COLLIDED WITH THE SUN 2 YEARS AGO". 1981, pp. Section 1, Page 11.

Orff, Eric. "New Hampshire Weasels- NH Fish And Wildlife". *Nhfishandwildlife.Com*, https://www.nhfishandwildlife.com/weasels.php.

Popova M. November 27, 1965: A Rare Recording of Stanley Kubrick's Most Revealing Interview. Brain Pickings. https://www.brainpickings.org/2013/11/27/jeremy-bernstein-stanley-kubrick-interview/. 2013.

Redfern, Nick. "A Saga of Extraterrestrial Dogmen | Mysterious Universe". *Mysterious Universe*, 2018, https://mysteriousuniverse.org/2018/11/a-saga-of-extraterrestrial-dogmen/.

Redfern, Nick. "Aliens: The "Hybrid Children" Controversy". *Mysterious Universe*, 2018, https://mysteriousuniverse.org/2018/12/aliens-the-hybrid-children-controversy/.

Ridge, Francis L. "Front Desk". *Nicap.Org*, 2019, http://www.nicap.org/madar.htm.

Ridge, Francis L. "MADAR UFO Detection Home Page". *Nicap.Org*, http://www.nicap.org/madar-1.htm?fbclid=IwAR1quabLfnEtcbjwnmP9ftnm-iFiLZUH2useFK03_uwnNatsFHA9m1hv9zQ.

Riley, Margaret et al. "Common Questions About Oppositional Defiant Disorder". *Aafp.Org*, 2016, https://www.aafp.org/afp/2016/0401/p586.html.

Schinella, Tony. "Did You See the UFO on Sunday?". *Nashua, NH Patch*, 2014, https://patch.com/new-hampshire/nashua/did-you-see-ufo-sunday-0.

Schinella, Tony. "More Pulsating UFO Orbs Reported In NH". *Bedford, NH Patch*, 2016, https://patch.com/new-hampshire/bedford-nh/more-pulsating-ufo-orbs-reported-nh.

Schinella, Tony. "More UFO Lights Seen Over Concord". *Concord, NH Patch*, 2015, https://patch.com/new-hampshire/concord-nh/more-ufo-lights-seen-over-concord.

Schinella, Tony. "UFO Update: Craft Was Seen in Concord, Boscawen". *Concord, NH Patch*, 2014, https://patch.com/new-hampshire/concord-nh/ufo-update-craft-was-seen-concord-boscawen.

Slevik, Nomar. *Otherworldly Encounters: Evidence of UFO Sightings and Abductions*. Llewellyn Worldwide, Ltd, 2018.

Stevens, Mike. "Granite Skies Interview Conducted by Nomar Slevik". New Market, New Hampshire & Kennebunk, Maine, 2019.

Strieber, Whitley. *Communion*. Beech Tree Books, 1985.

Tracy, Paula. "Rare Deer Spotted in Bristol". *WMUR.com*, 2015, https://www.wmur.com/article/rare-deer-spotted-in-bristol/5202540.

Vike, Brian. "Huge UFO Sighted - 1959 USAF SAC Base, Goose Bay, Labrador". *Sightings.com*, http://www.sightings.com/Archives/goosebay1959.html.

Woolley B.Sc., Rebecca. "Endometrial Scratching And IVF". *News-Medical.Net*, 2018, https://www.news-medical.net/health/Endometrial-Scratching-and-IVF.aspx.

ADDITIONAL WORKS BY NOMAR SLEVIK

DOCUMENTARIES (Available on Amazon Prime)
- Otherworldly Amor (writer, editor, director)
- Abducted New England (writer & co-director w/ Bill Brock)

BOOKS (Available wherever books are sold)
- Otherworldly Encounters: Evidence of UFO Sightings and Abductions
  Llewellyn Worldwide Publishing
- UFOs Over Maine: Close Encounters from the Pine Tree State
  Schiffer Publishing, Ltd.

PODCAST (Available on Apple Podcasts, Spotify & more)
- I Want to Believe: The Podcast

SLEVIK SOCIAL MEDIA
- Facebook – @NomarSlevikAuthor
- Twitter & Instagram – @nomarslevik

WEBSITES
- nomarslevik.bigcartel.com (Store)
- allmylinks.com/slevik

WORKS BY VALERIE LOFASO

BOOKS (Available on Amazon, Kindle, Nook, eBook & Google Play)
- Tangled Web of Friends: Book I - Summer Camp
- Tangled Web of Friends: Book II - The Witches of Fishkill Pond

LOFASO SOCIAL MEDIA
- Facebook – @ValerieLofaso
- Instagram – @valwrites17

GRANITE SKY SERVICES CREATED BY MIKE STEVENS

WEBSITE
- GraniteSky.Org

CONTACT
- graniteskyservices@gmail.com

GRANITE SKY SOCIAL MEDIA
- Facebook – @GraniteSky